Creative Wedding Keepsakes

By Donna Kooler

A LEISURE ARTS PUBLICATION

10   9   8   7   6   5   4   3   2   1

Library of Congress Cataloging-in-Publication Data
    Kooler, Donna
    Creative Wedding Keepsakes
    "A Leisure Arts Publication"

ISBN: 1-57486-286-3

Contributors

PRODUCED BY

PUBLISHED BY

If you have questions or comments
please contact:

LEISURE ARTS CUSTOMER SERVICE
P.O. Box 55595
Little Rock, AR 72215-9633
www.leisurearts.com

KOOLER DESIGN STUDIO, INC.
399 Taylor Blvd. Suite 104
Pleasant Hill, CA 94523
kds@koolerdesign.com

PRINTED IN THE U.S.A. BY
R.R. Donnelley & Sons, Co.

KOOLER DESIGN STUDIO

PRESIDENT: Donna Kooler
EXECUTIVE V.P.: Linda Gillum
VICE PRESIDENT: Priscilla Timm
EDITOR: Judy Swager
ILLUSTRATORS: Linda Gillum, Barbara Baatz
Sandy Orton, Nancy Rossi,
Jorja Hernandez
STAFF: Sara Angle, Jennifer Drake
Virginia Hanley-Rivett
Marsha Hinkson, Karen Million,
Char Randolph, Linnea Wiser

CREATIVE WEDDING KEEPSAKES

CREATIVE DIRECTOR: Donna Kooler
EDITORS: Jo Lynn Taylor, Judy Swager
BOOK DESIGN: Nancy Wong Spindler
WRITERS: Shelley Carda, Linda Gillum,
Basha Hanner, Ellaraine Lockie,
Chris Mitchell, Kit Schlich,
Lauren Fielder
COPY EDITOR: Kit Schlich
ILLUSTRATORS: Linda Gillum, Jo Lynn Taylor
PHOTOGRAPHERS: Dianne Woods, Berkeley, CA
Don Fraser, Berkeley, CA
PHOTO STYLISTS: Donna Kooler, Basha Hanner
DESIGNERS: Linda Gillum, Basha Hanner,
Ellaraine Lockie, Q. Stone Forbess
INDEXER: Joan Cravens
PROOFREADERS: Linnea Wiser, Sandy Orton

Contents

To Have and to Hold...

FROM THE MOMENT YOU SPEAK THE WEDDING VOWS AND
ever after, the sweet words will stir in your memories like the rustle of a wedding gown. So much joy, poignancy, exuberance and promise, all crowded into one glorious, all-too-short day. Such moments are far too precious to be hidden in the attics of memory, but can you preserve them for less than a king's ransom? Yes, you can.

Some things lend themselves willingly to the future. Textiles are among the easiest things to preserve. With a bit of care a delicate dress and veil can rustle around generations of happy brides.

More fleeting things can also be preserved for pennies. Your sun-filled bouquet can bloom for years in a place of honor, clear colors and smiling petals intact. But some things can only be preserved with self-restraint. Human nature being what it is, the top tier of your delectable wedding cake will vanish at a festive anniversary long before time consumes it.

Crisp invitations hold history in their snowy folds, yet paper can hold so much more than history. Transform scraps and fragments from plans and parties into luxurious hand-made papers, full of the tints, scents, and shining threads of your happiest days.

With a little planning and ingenuity the colors, tastes, and textures of your wedding can become something "to have and to hold"—and to share—long after the beautiful day has again become the stuff of dreams. ❧

Preserving Your Bouquet, Gown, and Cake

ONCE UPON A TIME THERE WAS A BEAUTIFUL PRINCESS BRIDE whose gown awaited her wedding day for a hundred years. Her beautiful flowers sat in stately beauty, year after year, ready for admiring glances and sighs. And a meltingly delicious cake stood frozen in time, until the pop of a celebratory cork and the blade of a silver knife should free it.

What wizard worked these wonders? No wizard, but the village dry cleaner, the village florist, and a clever caterer who understood the marvels of refrigeration and plastic wrap.

The same magic is available today to a clever bride who indulges in a bit of pre-nuptial preparation. You may provide the wedding dress for the bride a hundred years hence, but the bouquet and the cake are yours for the planning.

Ask the village florist to help you choose flowers which can hold up their heads to the passing years, then decide whether you want them to reside like swans under crystal, or as sentinels in your book of memories. Your florist will weave the spell, like ribbons, around the pick of the garden.

The village baker can help you select a cake rich enough to await your pleasure, which the clever caterer will whisk away before a crumb should stray. And on your anniversary, when you wave a silver knife over the cake to break the spell, the hand of greedy time may try to steal a morsel.

Your Bouquet

The wedding bouquet travels with you from the beginning to the close of your ceremony, as your expression of romance, signifying the beauty and elegance of the day in one, delicate bundle. The bouquet is a keepsake you will want to look back on frequently, so maintaining its beauty after the wedding is one way to keep your memories intact. Cut flower bouquets are highly perishable, but fortunately, there are measures you can take to preserve your bouquet's blossoms as a memento of your cherished day.

First, decide how you want to display your flowers after the wedding. Certain flowers are better suited to one treatment over another, so keep the types of flowers you are working with in mind when selecting the method. For a keepsake book or framed presentation, you want to choose your bouquet accordingly, as some flowers flatten better than others. Instructions for pressing flowers and a

list of potential blossoms appear later in this chapter. For a full, three-dimensional bouquet in a shadow box or glass display case, dry the flowers to preserve their original shape. Bear in mind that petal colors will probably change when dried: intense, bright colors may darken, medium shades may fade, and white and ivory often turn yellow.

For either the three-dimensional shadow box method or the book or framed presentation hang your bouquet (stem-end up) to dry as soon as possible after the ceremony. If this is not practical, enclose the bouquet in a large, sealed plastic bag for overnight storage. Blow some air into the bag, tie it securely, and place in the refrigerator. (Ask a bridesmaid or family member to take care of this for you, lest it slip your mind.) Avoid spraying the flowers with water, which can make them soggy and prone to mold, as well as more difficult to press or dry. Then, at your earliest convenience, remove the bouquet from the bag and hang it stem-end up to dry completely.

Some florists will freeze-dry your bouquet after the wedding for an additional cost. You may also find bouquet preservation services that specialize in maintaining bridal bouquets, from the drying stage to a complete reassembly of the blossoms into their original shape. You can expect to pay from $100 to $200 for this service, depending on the size of your bouquet. If you choose a specialty preservation service, make arrangements before the wedding. Because of the perishable nature of the bouquet, be precise in following the service's suggestions as to how to handle and store the bouquet after the ceremony.

PRESSING FLOWERS

Flowers that flatten easily and retain their appearance, such as pansies, violets, daisies, baby's breath, and Queen Anne's lace, will press well, as will those with a minimal number of petals, such as freesias and alstroemeria.

Cut the stem off just below each flower's base, then place the flowers on a sheet of paper, allowing for a minimum of an ⅛ inch between them. Include leaves and other greenery. Cover the flowers with another sheet of paper, and place them in a flower press or in the back of a heavy book. If you are pressing several layers of flowers, use extra sheets of paper between layers, and press them for at least two weeks. If you are using a flower press, follow the manufacturer's instructions.

Using a microwave can speed up the drying time, and produces almost instant results, as compared to the heavy book process. Some manufacturers have designed flower presses specifically for this process; however, you can also make your own by cutting two pieces of heavy cardboard approximately 10" square, and several pieces of white paper to match. Assemble layers of flowers, alternating with paper layers as described in the book or flower-press method above. Sandwich the flowers and paper layers between the pieces of cardboard with the paper on the bottom and top, forming a layer of protection between the flowers and cardboard. Then secure them snugly with rubber bands. Microwave the press for (approx.) two minutes on the low setting. Remove your homemade press and place a heavy book on top for about an hour, letting the contents cool.

BEST FLOWERS FOR DRYING

If you plan to dry your wedding bouquet's blossoms, give some thought to the flowers you select for the live bouquet. The following flowers dry attractively. If you would like to include a particular flower not on this list, talk to your florist.

Alstroemeria	Delphinium	Iris	Peony
Baby's Breath	Freesia	Lily	Queen Anne's Lace
Bouvardia	Gardenia	Lily-of-the-valley	Rose
Carnation	Heliotrope	Narcissus	Ranunculus
Chrysanthemum	Hyacinth	Orchid (except	Snapdragon
Daisy	Hydrangea	Cymbidium)	Tulip

DRYING FLOWERS

Rounded flowers such as roses, carnations, hydrangeas, delphiniums, and lilies are good candidates for dry three-dimensional arrangements. If you attempt to press them flat, they will become lumpy and unattractive.

As an alternative to hanging the bouquet, you can dry individual fresh flowers with silica gel, which maintains the flowers' shapes and colors quite well, avoiding the fading and discoloration that can occur. Look for silica gel at your local craft shop, and always wear a dust mask when working with this substance. Follow the steps below for preserving with silica.

PRESERVING FLOWERS WITH SILICA GEL

1. Find a large box with a tight-fitting lid. Cover the bottom of the box with approximately 1" of silica gel.
2. Remove the flowers you want to preserve from the bouquet, and trim the stems to within 1" of the flower base. Set each flower on the bed of silica, stem side down.
3. Gently spoon silica onto the flowers, filling and covering them without leaving air pockets. Cover the box and leave it alone for five days in an area that maintains a temperature under 80° Fahrenheit.
4. Test for "doneness" by uncovering a flower and touching it to see if it is cold. If it is cold, it isn't ready yet. Cover the flowers and check them

again in a day or two. The flowers are dry once they feel room-temperature to the touch. Keep them on the silica bed until you are ready to arrange them.

You have several options once the flowers have dried. You can glue them into an arrangement inside a shadow box, perhaps including other mementos from your wedding such as the invitation and select photographs. You can also create new arrangements with additional floral picks and florist tape, and then re-create your bouquet for a glass display case. Whatever method you choose, it is essential to keep the flowers dust-free.

Your Gown

Your bouquet, the décor, the reception, and the bridesmaids' dresses are all part of what makes your wedding complete. Your gown, however, is the focal point of the day, the culmination of months of planning and joyful preparation. You may hand it down to a daughter some day. You may simply preserve it for yourself, as a beautiful memento you can see and touch when you want to reminisce. Your gown is a time capsule that embodies the moment you married, and as such it has intrinsic, historical value. A garment this significant deserves thoughtful preservation. The same holds true of your headpiece and veil.

Textiles are subject to the destructive influences of light, humidity, dust, dirt, and chemicals, so there are precautions to take if you want your gown to look as lovely years from now as it did on your wedding day.

You may see articles and instructions refer to gown preservation as *garment archiving*. Regardless of the name, the process falls into three simple steps: cleaning, padding, and selecting a long-term storage method.

CLEANING YOUR GOWN

Your wedding is, after all, a celebration. So it should come as no surprise that you have to clean your gown before you store it. Stains from spillage while eating and drinking, the absorption of skin oils, hand lotion, make-up, perfume and perspiration all decay fabric over time, so cleaning your gown thoroughly is essential before you begin to pack it away.

Consider the style of your gown, the degree of embellishments such as lace and beadwork, and the fiber content of the fabric and trim when deciding on the best cleaning method for preservation.

The currently popular minimalist gown style with few or no embellishments is the easiest to archive. If you have such a gown and it is made of a washable synthetic such as polyester or nylon (not acetate or rayon) you can machine-wash it yourself, using a gentle setting and cool water. Avoid using fabric softener, starch and bleach, and hang the gown on a plastic hanger to dry. (Do not, however, plan to store the gown on a plastic hanger). If the gown has a small amount of beadwork, examine it closely to see if the beads are glued or sewn on. If they are glued, do not wash the gown in water. If the beads are sewn on, the gentle wash cycle should be fine, but you may want to consult with the dressmaker or manufacturer for specific guidelines.

If your gown is moderately adorned and made of silk, acetate, rayon, cotton, linen, or wool, have it professionally dry-cleaned. Expect a price similar to what you would pay for a formal evening gown. You should also dry-clean a gown with heavy lace and bead embellishments, as well as one with complex styling such as ruffles and an elaborate train. Most dry cleaners charge about $100 or more for the extra attention such a gown requires. You put a lot of time and money into your gown, so research the most reputable dry cleaners in your area and select one you would trust with your best. When you take your gown in for cleaning, be sure to tell the launderer how you intend to store the gown. Some dry cleaners offer to pack your gown in a box. Do not agree to a sealed box treatment, and be sure to read the following Long-term Storage section (below) before making any decisions.

Whichever cleaning method you choose, avoid ironing the gown if possible, as doing so contributes to the fabric's premature aging. In the case of fabric with heavy-set wrinkles, use a press-cloth on the clean garment to avoid touching the gown directly with the iron.

Take a moment to label your gown with your name, wedding date, and the garment's fiber content. Use a permanent fabric marker on a piece of cotton material or tape, then sew the label to a seam, preferably inside the skirt just above the hem. Years from now, this simple archiving touch could be a meaningful gesture to a new-generation bride.

PADDING

After many years in storage, your gown may form creases that you will never be able to iron out; aging fiber may even tear or crack along heavy crease lines. Fortunately, you can prevent hard creases by padding the garment with tissue paper before you store it. Standard gift-wrap tissue, which contains acids that eventually weaken fabrics, is not suitable for storage. Museum textile archivists recommend white, acid-free tissue. Use buffered tissue for cotton, linen, or synthetic gowns; use unbuffered for silk or wool.

When padding your gown, place the garment on a flat surface, so that it is entirely spread out. Then imagine your body inside the gown and simulate the same body shape and density with crumpled tissue. Crumple one sheet at a time to form the shape from multiple tissues. Then cover the gown itself with additional tissues. To protect a train about 12" or longer, form a tissue cylinder and roll the train around it, starting at the bottom, loosely rolling the pad toward the inside of the skirt.

LONG-TERM STORAGE

The difficult, time sensitive steps are over. Now you need to select the best method for storing your most cherished keepsake for years to come. You have two choices for storing your gown: boxing or hanging. Keep in mind that the fabric needs to breathe, and that the storage area must be dark and free from dampness and excessive heat, which rules out most basements and attics.

BOXING: This method is usually better than hanging. Boxing relieves the shoulder area from bearing the entire weight of the gown over time. Boxing is the obvious choice for strapless gowns or those with delicate straps.

Like the tissue you used for padding, acid-free boxes are strongly recommended even if your gown's fabric will not touch the actual box. Many cleaners include a box as part of the wedding gown dry cleaning service. Ask your cleaner if the box is acid-free; if it is not, purchase an acid-free box from another supplier. Do not accept a box with a cellophane window; the cellophane emits a vapor that turns white and ivory fabrics an unattractive yellow over time.

Considering the emotional and monetary value of your gown, be wary of any establishment that insists on returning your garment in a sealed box. Sealing prevents the fabric from breathing and keeps you from inspecting the cleaning job.

When you shop for a box, remember that padding significantly enlarges the gown. Full-length garment boxes are quite costly and take up a great amount of space, so consider shorter ones, in which you will have to fold the gown. As you box your gown, avoid creases by adding more crumpled tissue between the garment's layers.

HANGING: If you cannot obtain an acid-free box, storing your gown in a fabric bag is preferable to using a standard box that may have an acid content. Avoid using plastic or vinyl bags, which emit a harmful vapor similar to that of a cellophane window on a garment box. These materials may also create a greenhouse effect by trapping moisture, creating condensation which invites mildew and mold.

You can make a simple, fabric garment bag from a clean, white sheet, which you can customize to fit your gown. Make the bag large enough to prevent crushing by evaluating the size of the gown once you have padded it with tissue.

For the final step, your gown's hanger should be a wood or cloth-covered variety, not metal. Protect the gown's shoulders by wrapping cotton fabric padding around the top of the hanger. To spare a heavy gown's shoulder area from the stress of additional weight brought about from hanging, attach twill tape hanger loops from the inside of the waist area. Now that you have cleaned and properly stored your gown, you can rest assured your memories are secured.

Your Cake

Wedding folklore offers many customs to assure newlyweds' good luck and a happy, successful marriage. Saving the top tier of your wedding cake to enjoy on your first anniversary is one such tradition, designed to commemorate a milestone and symbolically remind you and yours to continue to nourish each other lovingly.

In the years predating refrigeration, the only practical choice for a couple was to bake and frost a dense cake such as fruitcake as the top tier, then wrap it up and store it in the larder until that landmark first anniversary. After twelve months on the shelf, these cakes were usually dry and tasteless. In contemporary days, fruitcake has fallen out of favor, and why not? There are so many other cake flavors and compositions to please the eye and palate. With the advantage of a freezer, a newlywed couple today can take advantage of a wide variety of cake choices and a greater opportunity than their great-grandmothers had to enjoy a still-tasty treat as they celebrate their first year together.

As you plan the top tier of your wedding cake, think in advance about which ingredients freeze best and which retain the cake's shape and flavor. You can select a top tier made from the same ingredients as the rest of the cake or choose a unique flavor for the top tier only. Discuss with your baker your plan to keep a portion of the cake to enjoy later. He or she will most likely tell you to avoid whipped cream frosting and custard filling. Buttercream, royal, fondant, ganache, or marzipan frosting, and a semi-firm filling such as jam or marmalade, curd, marzipan paste, or crushed nut paste are better choices.

Before your wedding day, let your caterer and food servers know that you would like them to whisk away the portion of cake you want to save, before they cut and serve the rest to guests. Improperly stored cake runs the risk of freezer burn, so be sure to have an air-tight, plastic container intended for freezer storage available.

After the reception, take the cake container home and place it in your freezer for 24 hours. (Better yet, entrust someone else with this task, as you will doubtlessly have other things to do). After the 24-hour period, remove the cake and wrap it snugly in plastic freezer wrap. Finally, place the wrapped cake back into the plastic container, and make sure the lid's seal is tight.

A day or two before your first anniversary take the cake container from the freezer, remove the plastic wrap, and then place it back in the container to defrost in the refrigerator. Make sure to have a bottle of champagne or sparkling cider on hand, and get ready to celebrate the first year of your new life together. *Bon appétit!* ♂

Memory Keeping

SCRAPBOOKS HOLD THE FRAGMENTS OF DREAMS FULFILLED or dreams to come; they are guidebooks to our shining moments. Mementos should be treated like the treasures they are—laid gently on smooth paper, dusted with sighs of happiness. Each memento preserved for our descendants gives another moment of life to us and to them, as shared joys live again.

Make an album worthy of your dreams. Cover it with lace, illuminate its pages with beautiful script and touches of gold, or with flowers and bits of sky. Do whatever makes the turn of each page an open door to the sweetest moments of your life. Fill it with bits of delight: colors, smiles, and photos of airborne bouquets; frosted lips and the napkin which wiped them clean for kisses. Nothing is too humble to awaken happy memories.

Or make a window on the past with a shadow box. A silk flower, a glove, and a folded invitation in a simple frame can recall the warm bliss of a summer afternoon. Memories of joyful times drift back like breezes.

Fortunately, aids to preservation are abundant, varied, and beautiful. Acid-free papers, decorative trims in every material, hue, and style make possible memories for any color scheme, any décor, and every room. If not yet, then soon… soon your life will be rich with images to save and savor. These are just the first of many. Gaze in serene contentment, or turn over the patchwork pages of happiness as you add to them again and again.

TOOLS AND MATERIALS

Everything you need to know about getting started in scrapbooking you learned in kindergarten. Just as when you were little, half the fun of scrapbooking lies in exploring and experimenting with a variety of new and interesting tools and implements. We've shown you just a few on these pages. Visit your local art supply and craft stores, or see Resources (page 94). The wealth of choices available today in papers, colors and textures is awesome, and you may have a hard time limiting your choices. Before purchasing your supplies, peruse this entire chapter for an overview. Read the information in the beige-colored boxes and view the sample pages for ideas.

PAGES AND PAPERS

For color and texture, paper is one of the most interesting and variable elements of your memory page display. Choose acid-free papers whenever possible. If you can't resist other products such as wrapping and specialty papers, use an archival spray-on product you can apply to non-archival papers. It creates a barrier to protect your memorabilia from the degenerative effects of acid and other harmful chemicals.

CARDSTOCK is the ideal choice for the actual pages of your memory book, and is also suitable for accents such as cutouts and photo matting or mounting.

VELLUM adds transparent elegance when used as overlays, in either solids or attractive patterns.

HANDMADE PAPERS come in a wonderful variety of colors, weights, and textures. You can even make your own (see page 75 for an introduction).

RICE AND MULBERRY PAPERS, from tissue-light to medium weight, add interesting texture to your pages and are particularly effective when trimmed with decorative-edge scissors.

CUTTING TOOLS

SCISSORS are essential for scrapbooking, and come in many specialty styles. Decorative-edge scissors create different effects on paper edges; deckle and antique edges are popular. Non-stick scissors are great for cutting stickers or tape because they are coated with a surface that repels the adhesive; they stay clean and don't tear up stickers. Spring-loaded scissors help alleviate fatigue when you cut multiple items such as stencils or small cutouts.

PAPER CUTTERS are designed to help you cut perfect, straight lines. The 12" length works on most cardstocks and vellums; the 9" trimmer is convenient for cropping photos. Each has a grid for accurate measuring and easy-to-replace blades. Fiskar has a good line called *Personal Trimmers* (see Resources).

CUTTING "SYSTEMS" consist of a template with cutouts in specific shapes and various sizes. They are easy to use, come in a variety of shapes, and are available wherever scrapbooking supplies are sold. *The Creative Memories Cutting System,* available through home parties and online (see Resources), conveniently cuts a wide range or oval and circle sizes; it has three blades, each with guides that fit into a grooved template, which results in precisely cut shapes in different size increments.

PUNCHES come in an array of shapes and sizes so you can cut paper cutouts for embellishment. Flower shapes are popular and appealing. Corner Rounders let you trim corners to create a softer look to your layout.

CRAFT AND UTILITY KNIVES feature replaceable, razor-fine blades for precision free-hand trimming.

TWEEZERS are useful for picking stickers off the backing paper and good for holding small punch-outs as you position and glue them to the page.

TEMPLATES AND STENCILS are invaluable for cutting paper or photos into shapes or to add embossing, graphics or lettering to a layout. Simply window-shopping for templates will inspire creative ideas.

From upper left: Sticker strips (1), paper cutter (2), Creative Memories cutting system (3), adhesives (4), paper punches (5), specialty papers (6), pens and burnisher (7), tapes (8), decorating chalk (9), stickers (10), stencil (11), shape-cutting system (12).

ADHESIVES

Serious scrapbooking requires an assortment of adhesives. Some—like tacky glue, double-stick tape, tape runners, photo tape, glue pens, and spray adhesives—are simple and invisible. Others—stickers, photo squares, and photo mounting corners—are meant to be seen and add interest to a page. Again, as for anything that will contact an irreplaceable memento, be sure your chosen adhesive is acid-free.

LIQUID GLUE such as tacky glue and matte medium are a crafter's standby, and works for basic gluing jobs on many surfaces.

GLUE PENS are ideal for photos and small pieces such as cutouts and punched paper.

TAPES vary to fit specific needs. Photo tape is very sticky and not repositionable, but it's great for adhering heavy paper and photomat to album pages. Photo splits are small rectangles of double-sided tape that can be used on any papers; they have a paper backing tape that allows you to reposition the item before you expose the adhesive. Tape runners are little rectangles of double-sided tape that can be placed one at a time or in a line, depending on how much you need (about ½" of tape in each corner of a photo is sufficient to hold permanently). Photo squares (½" pre-cut squares) can be applied one at a time.

PHOTO MOUNTING CORNERS, popular with scrapbookers for years, are now available in an array of decorator colors, including metallics. You'll find them useful to mount a photo that you may want to remove at a later time, and as a decorative accent even if your photo is attached with another adhesive.

STICKERS are the most dramatic of all the adhesives because they add immediate visual impact to your pages. They come in all sizes, colors, and themes, from formal to funny. Use them to affix lightweight elements on your page or simply to add embellishment.

STICKER STRIPS are slender 12" lengths of stickers you can cut as desired to mount and frame photos or enhance a layout by adding a border.

WRITING TOOLS

For photo captions, headlines and journal entries, you'll want to investigate a variety of writing implements and other art media.

PENS AND MARKERS come in a fabulous variety of tip shapes and sizes as well as a rainbow of colored and metallic inks. Gel pens are effective on dark papers.

DECORATING CHALK, colored pencils and crayons will bring out your best artistic efforts. Use them to add color to mats, cutouts, punches, and embossed images. Chalk (applied with cotton swabs) is safe for albums but shouldn't be used directly on photos; after applying, you may want to "fix" it with finishing spray so it won't smear.

BURNISHING AND EMBOSSING TOOLS help you create raised lettering and other decorative effects.

GETTING STARTED

With rolls and rolls of photographs and just as many keepsakes from this magical beginning of your lives together, where do you start? The first step is to determine the size of album you want to use. (See page 62 for some ideas.) The album's dimensions and page count will dictate how many pictures you will be able to work with, per page and overall—the smaller the album, the fewer pictures you can use. The most popular size is the 12" x 12" album.

Top to bottom: spring-loaded, decorative-edge, and non-stick scissors.

Sort your photos in chronological order and keep them in a photo storage box until you need them. Storing them in the envelopes from the processor is acceptable for short-term keeping. A storage box provides a convenient way to find the pictures you are looking for and keeps them within easy reach as you're working. Also, keep the negatives handy in case you want duplicates later. Store larger photos in containers from your local craft store.

Next, decide how you will present your content. One logical approach is to arrange the sections by the order of events, starting with your engagement, then to your showers, wedding, and honeymoon. Or, you could start with your wedding and then work backward to the showers and engagement. Your album will reflect the sentiment of your special day, so when planning your pages, consider what you want to express to those who will view it.

CAREFUL PRESERVATION

Take care to use only high-quality, acid-free, photo-safe products. Many products on the market claim to be archival, but check to be sure they are also specifically acid-free and photo-safe. Because you will devote so much thoughtful effort to your album, you'll want to make certain it is a lasting heirloom you can pass down to future generations.

PAGE SLEEVES AND PHOTO SLEEVES, made of plastic, will protect your pages. Buy those specified as archival.

THE ART OF CROPPING

Artful photo cropping enhances the subject by eliminating unimportant or undesirable parts of the photo. It can be useful for candid shots with busy backgrounds, flares from flashes, and for those in which the photographer left subjects' heads out of the frame! Use discretion when cropping, though. Keep in mind that the background can serve as a frame that enhances your photo. That car in the background may be fun to see in twenty years. The trees

and shrubs may be much taller or even gone when you revisit your honeymoon destination. Sometimes the background information is as much a part of your wedding archive as the subject in each shot. Refer to scanning and copying (page 45) for more information. ✌

WHY ARCHIVAL MATERIALS?

Photographs are fragile mementos that damage easily when exposed to harsh elements. The way you handle and display them will lengthen or considerably shorten their lives.

The acid content in paper and inks can discolor the photos, causing them to become brittle. When you place your photos in albums with "magnetic" pages that allow you the freedom of placement without extra adhesives, the images can fade, turn yellow, and stick to the pages after just a few years.

When creating your scrapbook, consider it a heritage to pass on to future generations. You should craft this heirloom with the best materials available—those that will prolong the life of your treasured memories. Use only acid-free, lignin-free cardstock or treat non-acid-free items with products that render them safe; journal with permanent, photo-safe pens, and finally, use page protectors on all of your finished album pages.

Pre-Wedding Memory Pages

Invitation to Share the Joy

Nature's Blessings

Precious Pearls

DEPENDING ON HOW YOU decide to organize your memory book, you may want to start with those preliminary events that lead up to the wedding. However, you may want to have three or more separate books to commemorate the separate events—engagement party, showers and rehearsals, the wedding itself, the reception, the honeymoon, etc. Whatever you decide, most of the pages in this section have been designed around preliminary events—invitations and showers. This could be the beginning of a tradition that carries on through all the joyous events of your life! ∾

INVITATION TO SHARE THE JOY *(upper left)*
SUPPLIES: cardstock, various patterned papers, invitation, photo, shape cutter, flower punches, doily, ribbon rose, ribbon, adhesive

An Invitation to Tea

Tea and Treasures

INSTRUCTIONS

Mount the invitation on a large sheet of pinstriped patterned paper. Mount an oval-cut picture on an oval of patterned paper and embellish with flower punches (see Punched Flowers, page 43) cut in half. A Battenberg lace doily, ribbon rose and sheer ribbon at the top corner help to soften the dark, striped paper.

NATURE'S BLESSINGS *(page 22)*

SUPPLIES: embossed paper, photo, photo sleeve, photo mounting corners, narrow patterned ribbon, dried pressed leaves and flowers, announcement with bow, adhesive

INSTRUCTIONS

Mount the announcement on embossed paper. Mount your photo in a protective sleeve with photo mounting corners and position it over the announcement. Arrange the dried leaves and flowers around it. Adhere the ribbon 1" from the top and bottom edges.

PRECIOUS PEARLS *(page 22)*

SUPPLIES: cardstock, patterned paper, vellum, photo, invitation, narrow ribbon, flat pearls, tacky glue

INSTRUCTIONS

Mount your photos on gold paper and arrange photos and invitation on a sheet of patterned paper. Print a piece of vellum cut the size of the printed invitation with the first names of the bride and groom, and place at an opposing angle for variety. Glue a narrow gold ribbon to the edge of the paper, and glue flat pearls to the corners.

AN INVITATION TO TEA *(upper left)*

SUPPLIES: various cardstocks, patterned papers, embossed paper, mulberry paper, invitation, photo mounting corners, chalk, shape cutter, foam spacers, colored pencils, stickers, decorative scissors, ribbon, adhesive

INSTRUCTIONS

Cut patterned paper to the size of your album page. Use shape cutter to cut striped paper and solid cardstock. Mount invitation on shaped papers, using photo mounting corners. Punch two holes through all layers and thread ribbon through fold as shown. Glue this assemblage onto patterned paper.

For accents, cut teapot motif from embossed paper. Use decorative scissors to cut a circle of mulberry paper; cut a slightly larger circle of cardstock using shape cutter. Stack and adhere these three elements together using a foam spacer for teapot (see photo) and glue to shaped area above invitation. Shade teapot with colored chalk. Draw a cup, saucer, heart, and small rectangle on cardstock and striped paper, and cut out. Embellish cup and saucer with stickers. Attach these elements to the vellum layer of the invitation.

TEA AND TREASURES *(page 23)*

For a variation of An Invitation to Tea, add some photos to the materials and use an understated, patterned paper to create the background. Cut a wide strip of floral paper and position it horizontally across the middle of the page. Double-mount the photos with cardstock and mulberry paper cut with the decorative scissors. Add a circle cut out of striped patterned paper and mulberry paper. Enhance the page with three more teapots using foam spacers.

INVITATION IN TOILE *(page 25)*

SUPPLIES: cardstock, patterned papers, vellum invitation, stickers, foam spacer, decorative scissors, photos, shape cutters, spray adhesive

INSTRUCTIONS

Use pink patterned paper the size of your album page.

USING COLOR

You carefully select your wedding colors to connect the style or theme of your big day, and to compliment one another. As with your wedding, color is essential to a great looking scrapbook. So you want to choose just a few colors to create an elegant look for your book's pages. Choosing colors that enhance photos is as important as the photos themselves. Contrast, texture and highlighting are all features that you can incorporate into your wedding album.

✎ Use double photo mounts and mulberry paper to accent with color and give importance to photos.

✎ Patterned paper and hand-colored embellishments create an exciting theme page.

✎ Monochromatic pages recreate the soft mood of the wedding, while an elegant white on white relies on texture and shadows for interest.

✎ Use nature's bright colors, especially green, to tie the pictures of an outdoor wedding together, and pick up the same shades for complementary lettering.

✎ Enhance black-and-white and sepia-toned photos by repeating the tones, leaving out bright colors. Heavy contrast on double mats makes photos jump off the page.

Invitation in Toile

Please join us for an
Entertainment Shower & Luncheon
honoring
Shadia Crandall
Wednesday, May 9th
12:00
Claremont Country Club
Blue Room
5295 Broadway Terrace
Oakland

Mount the vellum invitation on green-striped and light-patterned paper and center it on the pink paper. Place a sticker at the top backed with a foam spacer for depth. Add another sticker to the bottom, if desired.

A CHARMING LOCATION *(right)*

For a facing page to Invitation in Toile, add some photos to the materials. Crop and mount photos with colors that coordinate with the facing page's patterned paper. Cut the patterned paper around the edges with decorative-edge scissors. Finish the page with stickers mounted on foam spacers.

A Charming Location

Wrapped With Love

Shower of Gifts From A to Z

larger than photos. Arrange photocopy and mounted photos onto the vellum and attach using adhesive.

WRAPPED WITH LOVE *(above)*

SUPPLIES: various cardstocks, patterned vellum, color photocopy of gift packages, photos, shape cutter, adhesive

INSTRUCTIONS

Trim vellum to fit album page. Use the shape cutter to cut the photos into various shapes (see photo). Mount each onto colored cardstock and trim cardstock slightly

SHOWER OF GIFTS FROM A TO Z *(above)*

SUPPLIES: cardstock, lettered vellum, invitation, photos, photo mounting corners, adhesive

INSTRUCTIONS

To commemorate an alphabet-themed shower, choose lettered vellum for album page. Lightly glue the bottom of the invitation to the bottom of the page, and casually arrange photos around it, allowing the invitation to overlap photos. Add mounting corners to the photos and attach all elements using adhesive.

DESIGNING YOUR PAGES: COMPOSITION

A memory album page communicates an important event visually. Design, or composition, supports the visual message. Good composition, (a pleasing arrangement of shapes) makes a memory page interesting and comfortable to view. Elements of composition include center of interest, balance, movement, contrast, value and shape.

CENTER OF INTEREST

The center of interest is where you want to draw the viewer's attention. Compositions can have a very strong center of interest (page 59), or more subtle areas of interest (pages 54, 55). Highlights and accents can create a center of interest. These may include embellishments such as stickers, ribbons or buttons, or could be color accents or areas of strong contrast (pages 22, 35, 56).

BALANCE AND MOVEMENT

Balance must be present in a composition to make the viewer feel at ease, whether a composition is symmetrical (equal use of space on opposite sides) or asymmetrical (unequal use of space). An "off balance" composition results from having too much visual weight in one area. Leading the eye through the composition creates movement and links one element to another (pages 28–32).

CONTRAST, VALUE AND SHAPE

Contrast, value and shape will also affect your design. An area of strong contrast, such as black against white, will draw the viewer's attention. Very dark values tend to come forward and will also tend to dominate a page. Shapes can add movement and interest. Using a few different shapes and repeating shapes for continuity will create an interesting look. On the other hand, too many different shapes will give your album a "busy" look.

The examples of compositions below may help you find new ways of expressing your ideas. Make thumbnail drawings (small, simple sketches) to experiment with moving your shapes and embellishments around into interesting arrangements. Include drawn lines for lettering to indicate how it will affect the composition.

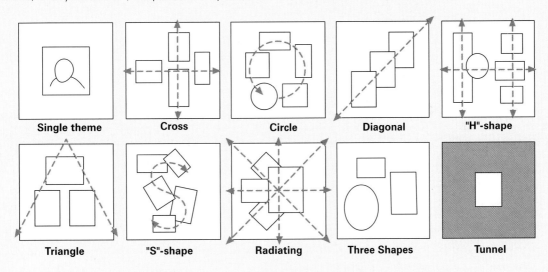

Single theme   Cross   Circle   Diagonal   "H"-shape

Triangle   "S"-shape   Radiating   Three Shapes   Tunnel

Wedding Memory Pages

Lanterns Light the Way

YOUR CREATIVE MEMORY PAGES ARE ONLY limited by your imagination—what better time than now to let loose that latent artistic talent of yours! Decide on an album first. Choosing an Album (on page 62) has tips for selecting the one that is just right for your needs. Once you've chosen a size, there are dozens of creative ways to design those pages! Of course, you aren't limited to just one album—scrapbooking can be habit forming! ✄

LANTERNS LIGHT THE WAY

SUPPLIES: cardstock, corrugated paper, shape cutter, decorating chalk, gold cording, foam spacers, photos, invitation, sheer ribbon, gold and black heat-stamp embossing supplies, mulberry paper, handmade paper, heart punches, small hole punch, adhesive

INSTRUCTIONS

An Asian theme with the paper lanterns used at the reception inspires this album's design. Choose cardstock for the pages that picks up the color of the lanterns. Cut graduating sizes of circles out of corrugated paper and use decorating chalk to adjust the color if necessary. Add

Lanterns Light the Way, continued

cording tied through a small punched hole and elevate the lanterns with foam spacers. Showcase the invitation with a sheer ribbon on which a gold, heat-stamp embossed Asian character has been centered. Anchor the ribbon with a strip of colored mulberry paper and add heart and flower punches. Mount a gold-lined envelope containing a photo of the newlyweds.

Continue the color scheme on subsequent pages, and repeat the heat-embossed Asian characters, lanterns and flower punches where you need to add a spot of interest or hide a photo mistake.

For the journaling boxes, mat strips of mulberry paper on cardstock and mount in position. Letter the titles top

to bottom to emulate Asian calligraphy. (For more about lettering, see page 49.)

Trim the photos in a variety of shapes and mount on coordinating cardstock, repeating the circle and rectangle shapes; then use handmade papers at the edges of the pages to unify the elements.

Create the fan by cutting colored paper into ¾" x 6" strips and then cutting them on the diagonal. Adhere the pieces to a ⅛ circle template, so you can move the fan around before you mount it permanently. Hand-cut paper lilies and edge with gold heat-embossing. Use flower punches (see page 43) of different sizes and colors for visual appeal.

Lantern Wedding Pocket

LANTERN WEDDING POCKET *(above)*

SUPPLIES: cardstock, heavy handmade paper, ribbon, gold and black decorative paper, heat-stamp embossing supplies, flower punches, double-sided tape, tacky glue, wide sheer ribbon

INSTRUCTIONS

This page was designed to be a keepsake pocket for invitations, notes, and other paper memorabilia. Follow the instructions to Create a Note Card Pocket (right) and make a large envelope out of heavy handmade paper. Wrap the envelope with a sheer ribbon adhered to the back using double-sided tape, and tied in front.

Balance the page with a heat-embossed character on gold and black decorative paper at bottom left and coordinating flower punches (page 43) at upper right attached with tacky glue.

CREATE A NOTE CARD POCKET

SUPPLIES: heave handmade paper, tacky glue

1. Start with a piece of decorative paper 26¼" x 6¾". We used rice paper.
2. Lightly pencil the guidelines as indicated below.

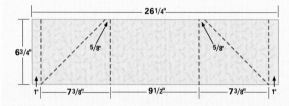

3. Fold the 1" tabs toward the back.

4. Crease the diagonal fold lines toward you. Fold the inside right vertical fold line to the inside of the pocket and repeat with the left side.

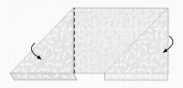

5. Fold the 1" tabs to the backside of the pocket and glue down.

pocket front

pocket back

EMBELLISHING YOUR PAGES

At the heart of your memory book adventure is the joy of embellishing the pages as you see fit. A visit to your local craft store will dazzle you with hundreds of decorative materials to enhance the photos and memorabilia from your wedding.

Consider meaningful items you might already have at hand. Look for personal embellishments to dress the pages of your album, such as honeymoon souvenirs, jewelry (new and vintage), shells, feathers, dried flowers and leaves, paper ephemera, and pretty much anything that you can attach to a surface. It is fun to watch out for all the wonderful "found" objects around you—things around your house, at flea markets and specialty shops, and in nature, whether from the forest, the beach, or your own backyard.

It's easy to get carried away when selecting colors, textures, and patterns. If you find yourself overdoing it, remember that your photos are the real stars of the memory book, and too much embellishment can detract from their beauty. Ideally, embellishment picks up clues from the photos themselves—the colors of attendants' dresses or reception decorations, the formality of a cathedral ceremony, or the rustic charm of an outdoor party.

SPECIALTY PAPER

Lively mixes of patterns and textures make appealing frames for your photos, and paper is one of the easiest ways to achieve this. Art and craft stores are brimming with exciting paper styles and patterns (see page 19). Look in the scrapbooking sections, but check out the gift-wrapping aisle, too. You can also dress up plain paper by adding embossed motifs or even lightweight fabric affixed with spray adhesive. There are endless possibilities of computer-printed paper motifs (see page 26 for a stunning example).

SURFACE DECORATION

Add visual interest and decorative motifs directly onto paper using paint, add decorating chalk, stencils, glitter and rubber stamps with colored inks. For journal lettering, try pens, markers, painting, and rub-on alphabets. Beautiful fonts from your computer instantly provide lettering when printed from the new generation of color printers, which can take the guesswork out of journaling. (Read about journaling ideas on page 37.)

FLAT TRIMS

Stickers are one of the most popular scrapbooking trims, and you are sure to find ones that complement your theme. Glue-on embellishments include shapes such as lettering and flowers created by paper punches, and pre-cut photo mats. Flat ribbon and lace make attractive borders and accents.

DIMENSIONAL TRIMS

Here's where you can pull out all the stops! Create glamour with glued-on pearls, rhinestones, and charms. Add interesting textures with punched and folded paper flowers. Ribbon flowers—either purchased or handmade from wired ribbon, along with velvet or sheer "skeletonized" leaves—lend themselves to bridal themes.

Shimmering Leaves Invitation

SHIMMERING LEAVES

The five pages in this series were inspired by the silver-dot embossed paper that makes up the background mat of the simple white invitation, above. Draw from the same supplies for all five album pages.

SUPPLIES: cardstock, silver-dot embossed paper, silver foil paper, photos, photo sleeves, invitation, mounting corners, sticker strips, skeletonized leaves, patterned vellum, shape cutter, white ribbon, double-stick tape, dot paint, adhesive

A Time to Rejoice

INSTRUCTIONS

FOR SHIMMERING LEAVES *(page 34)*

Use silver mounting corners, and center the invitation on the silver-dot embossed paper. Mat this onto two squares of offset silver foil papers. Mount the assemblage onto a black album page, and use silver pinstripe stickers to outline the edges. Finish with a white bow over two silver leaves.

FOR A TIME TO REJOICE *(above)*

The second page carries on the dot theme with a dot-printed vellum paper. Use a neutral cardstock for the album page. Mount the photo on two layers of cardstock and center them on the page. Cut a circle out of the middle of a square of dot-printed vellum and position it over the photo, framing the subjects in the circle. Tape the vellum in place with double-stick tape, then finish with a white bow to conceal the tape.

Shining Moments

FOR SHINING MOMENTS *(above)*

Mount the photos on pastel cardstock, and offset them on silver foil squares. Extend the theme of the silver dot embossed paper by adding decorative swashes with dot paint in the upper left (for a left-hand page). Angle journaling boxes to display written details of your wedding (see Journaling, page 37, and The Art of Lettering, page 49). Add a silver leaf to continue the reference to the invitation on page 34.

FOR TO LOVE AND BE LOVED... *(page 37)*

Mirror the Shining Moments page by repeating the treatment of the photos, silver dots, and journaling box. To add variety to the symmetrical composition, silhouette-cut the lower right-hand photo of the cake. Mount the cutout on black paper to enhance the image of the cake and make it come forward.

To Love and Be Loved...

JOURNALING

It is natural to want to focus on photos, but keeping a written record of the event is one of the most important aspects of making a scrapbook. This record should include full names of people shown, locations, dates (including the year), and some of the emotions experienced. Use sticker letters, calligraphy, or computer-generated lettering to journal, but consider also including at least some handwriting. Even if your penmanship isn't letter-perfect, it's a part of who you are, and should be included in your scrapbook. Or, enlist the help of a close friend whose writing you admire. Your children and grandchildren will appreciate your personal thoughts alongside the photos.

A Kiss Marks the Beginning

FOR A KISS MARKS THE BEGINNING *(above)*
In the final page of the Shimmering Leaves series,
choose grey cardstock as the album page. Use photo
mounting corners, and center the photo on silver-dot
embossed paper, then mount on black to frame. Mount
the assemblage on the grey cardstock.

WHITE LACE THEMED ALBUM *(right)*

You may want to set the theme of your album with a cover that introduces the elements of the pages inside. This cover features the scattered flowers on the following pages and adds the interest of a lace handkerchief to cover just the front of the purchased album. See page 63 for instructions on how to make it.

White Lace Album Cover

PHRASES OF LOVE...

In the beginning…

As we begin our life together…

To love and be loved is the greatest gift of all

Bless our wedding

With this ring I thee wed

From this day forward…

How do I love thee? Let me count the ways

I would be friends with you and have your love

God's greatest gift is love

I love you

The world is full of beauty when the heart is full of love

Love is sweet

Though I am different from you, we were born involved in one another —Tau Ch'ien

To love is to place our happiness in the love of another

Love cometh like sunshine after rain —Shakespeare

Love conquers all

Grow old along with me; the best is yet to be

Marriage is the golden ring in a chain, whose beginning is a glance and whose ending is eternity —Kahlil Gibran

Thou art my beloved

This ring is round and hath no end, so is my love unto my friend

Love is patient, love is kind

Love to live and live to love

Love one another, for he that loveth another hath fulfilled the law —Romans 13:8

Love makes the world go round

Love knows no bounds

Love is blind

Here's to you both, a beautiful pair, we celebrate your love affair

Mon amour

Sealed with a kiss

Lilies and Lace

LILIES AND LACE *(above)*

SUPPLIES: various cardstocks, embossed paper, rice paper, precut oval embossed mat, photo, decorative scissors, foam spacers, punches, tacky glue, foam core, burnishing tool, tracing paper

INSTRUCTIONS

Choose white embossed paper for the album page. Adhere the bride's photo into the oval of the precut mat, then add eight foam spacers to the back at the corners and sides. Use decorative scissors to cut rectangles of rice paper and white cardstock larger than the photo mat, and mount them together. Add eight foam spacers to the back of the largest rectangle; center and adhere them to the album page. Center and mount the matted photo over the rice paper using the spacers.

FOR EACH LILY:

Copy patterns on page 41, using tracing paper; cut one of each pattern from white, yellow, or green cardstocks.

Use the burnishing tool to emboss the paper cutouts. Place the pieces, right side down, on foam core and run the embossing tool about 1/16" inside the edge. Use a consistent, even pressure.

Turn the lily base and short stem pieces right side up and burnish veins (indicated by red dashed lines on patterns).

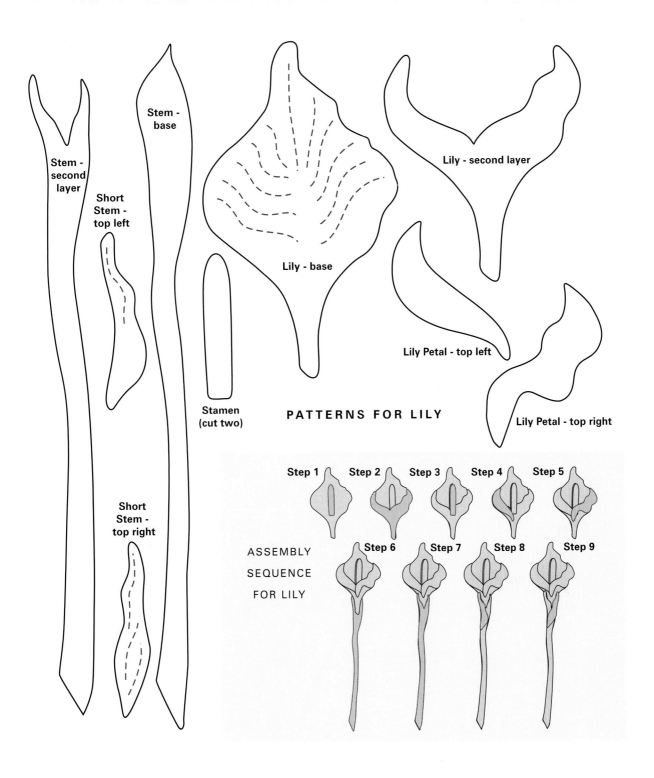

Stem - second layer

Stem - base

Short Stem - top left

Short Stem - top right

Stamen (cut two)

Lily - base

Lily - second layer

Lily Petal - top left

PATTERNS FOR LILY

Lily Petal - top right

ASSEMBLY SEQUENCE FOR LILY

Step 1   Step 2   Step 3   Step 4   Step 5

Step 6   Step 7   Step 8   Step 9

Refer to the illustration above for the order in which to assemble the lily. Step 1: Glue first stamen to the lily base. Follow the sequence in the illustration, gluing the second lily layer in place (Step 2). Position second stamen (Step 3) so that the top just covers the top of the first stamen. Attach it in place with a foam spacer centered underneath. Place left top petal into position with a centered foam spacer (Step 4). Use the tip of a toothpick to place glue at both the top and the bottom of the petal, and glue in place. Repeat for right top petal (Step 5). Follow steps 6–9 to glue stem layers.

Make three lilies, and position them gracefully between the layers of the mounted and lifted photo assembly.

Armful of Lilies

ARMFUL OF LILIES *(above)*

SUPPLIES: embossed paper, heart-shaped photo mounting punch, flower punches, photo, pearl beads, silk ribbon, small heart stickers, purchased lily favor, scoring stylus, tacky glue

INSTRUCTIONS

Choose an embossed white paper for the album page. Cut a rectangle of colored cardstock ½" larger on all sides than photo. Punch the corners using the heart-shaped photo mounting punch, and insert the photo. Use stickers to add small contrasting hearts at the corners. Wrap a purchased lily favor in white ribbon and tie with lavender ribbon bows. Glue it at an angle over the photo. Create the scattered flowers following the directions for Punched Flowers on page 43, and glue them to the mat with tacky glue.

FROM THIS DAY FORWARD *(page 43)*

SUPPLIES: embossed paper, heart-shaped photo mounting punch, flower punches, photo, pearl beads, gold pen, calligraphy pen with colored ink, tacky glue

INSTRUCTIONS

Choose an embossed white paper for the album page. Mount the photo on white cardstock ⅛" larger than photo, with a triangle above the photo to simulate the look of an envelope. Add a phrase (see Phrases of Love…, page 39) using a calligraphy pen. Refer to the The Art of Lettering, page 49. Cut two shapes of cardstock larger than the mounted photo. Punch the corners using the heart-shaped photo mounting punch, and insert the mounted photo. Use a gold pen to accent the edges. Create the scattered flowers following the directions for Punched Flowers on page 43, and glue them to the mat with tacky glue.

From This Day Forward

PUNCHED FLOWERS

SUPPLIES: lightweight cardstock, flower-shaped paper punches in two sizes, scoring stylus, tacky glue, pearl beads

INSTRUCTIONS

1. Using paper punches, punch out flower shapes in two sizes.

2. On the front of the larger cutout, score between each petal and from the middle outer edge to the center, using the small end of a stylus.

3. Gently fold all petals upward for a three-dimensional effect.

4. Glue the smaller flowers into the bowls of the larger flowers with a drop of tacky glue.

6. Glue a small pearl with a drop of tacky glue into the bowl of the smaller flower.

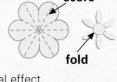

Seashell Mementos

SEASHELL MEMENTOS *(above)*

SUPPLIES: cardstock, patterned paper, photo, page sleeve, photo mounting corners, invitation, memorabilia, memorabilia pocket, decorative scissors, stick-on letters, skeletonized leaves, tacky glue

INSTRUCTIONS

Choose a patterned paper for the album page. Mount the invitation at the upper left. Use decorative scissors to cut a rectangle larger than the photo. Mount the photo using photo mounting corners. Glue mounted photo at an angle over the invitation. Glue memorabilia in the center, overlapping photo and invitation. Use a memorabilia pocket for small, loose materials. Finish the page with a title in adhesive letters. Insert into a page sleeve.

SURROUNDED BY FLOWERS *(page 45)*

SUPPLIES: cardstock, photo, page sleeve, shape cutter, corner punch, pressed dried flowers, adhesive, matte medium

INSTRUCTIONS

Select a dark cardstock for the album page. Trim contrasting cardstock ¼" smaller on all sides than the album page, and use a punch to cut out the corners. With a shape cutter, cut out an oval window to frame the photograph. Follow the steps for pressing flowers on page 11. When dry, arrange flowers around oval opening, and glue in position with matte medium under and over flowers as in *decoupage*. Mat the photo, and use adhesive to attach to album page. Use a page sleeve to protect the assemblage.

Scanning and Copying

Original mementos that were a part of your special event are treasures you'll certainly want to keep intact, so working with these precious items can be limiting. If you have a computer and scanner, scanning photos and other memorabilia gives you greater control and more freedom to explore page layouts. By simply changing the size of an object in a photo you can make arrangements more dramatic and might even give the viewer more information about the event. If you don't have a computer, a good color copier that enlarges and reduces can provide endless options: repetition, changes of scale, or enlargements for backgrounds.

Frame a special photo with a wreath of scanned flowers that duplicate the color and beauty of the wedding-day blossoms. Place actual fresh flowers on a scanner or copier and cover with white paper. Scan the image, reduce the size, and print (using acid-free photo paper) as many copies as you need to create the design. Use foam spacers to adhere cutouts of flowers on different layers, for a more three-dimensional look.

There is no limit to the types of items that you can scan. The possibilities are as boundless as the imagination, or at least the size of your scanner. For spotless scans, keep the glass on the scanning bed clean and never place anything on it that might scratch or damage the surface.

Surrounded by Flowers

Framed in Beauty

FRAMED IN BEAUTY *(above)*

SUPPLIES: embossed paper, shape cutter, photo, flowers printed on acid-free photo paper, foam spacers, adhesive

INSTRUCTIONS

To create this alternative to Surrounded by Flowers, use embossed paper with an oval cut out of center, but replace the dried flowers with scanned or copied fresh flowers. Reduce the size to fit the oval, and print out on acid-free paper. Cut shapes; use foam spacers for 3-D lift.

Silver Splendor

Peach Bouquet

SILVER SPLENDOR *(above)*

SUPPLIES: cardstock, decorative paper, silver paper, mulberry paper, ribbon bow, photo, photo mounting corners, shape cutter, invitation, vellum, double-stick tape, decorative-edge scissors, silver cabochon, adhesive, tacky glue

INSTRUCTIONS

Cut black embossed cardstock ½" smaller than the album page. Use photo mounting corners to mount the invitation on the cardstock. With the oval shape cutter, cut the photo and two ovals larger than the photo from silver and mulberry papers. Trim the edges of the middle oval using decorative edge scissors. Glue ovals together, then glue to a piece of vellum cut to fit the center of the invitation. Tape to the top of the invitation. Glue a ribbon bow to the top of the photo and embellish with a silver cabochon. Attach the black cardstock unit to the decorative paper by cutting a slit in each corner and securing with a small piece of tape behind the slit.

PEACH BOUQUET *(above)*

SUPPLIES: cardstock, patterned paper, silver paper, mulberry paper, ribbon, photos, photo mounting corners, spray adhesive, rose sticker

INSTRUCTIONS

Choose a dark patterned paper for the album page. Mount the photo on mulberry paper using photo mount corners, then adhere to a light-colored cardstock cut 2" longer than the mulberry paper. Mount the assembly on a silver paper cut ⅝" smaller than the album page. Use a sticker to hold a trimmed ribbon at the corner.

SUMPTUOUS CELEBRATION *(above)*

SUPPLIES: See Peach Bouquet, page 46

INSTRUCTIONS

As a variation on Peach Bouquet, use the same papers, but center the mulberry paper on the cardstock to unify the reception photos. The rosebud sticker adds a touch of continuity.

VINTAGE GETAWAY *(right)*

SUPPLIES: See Peach Bouquet, page 46

For another variation with the same papers, rotate the mulberry paper to create a diamond shape, and add a ribbon sticker on top.

Vintage Getaway

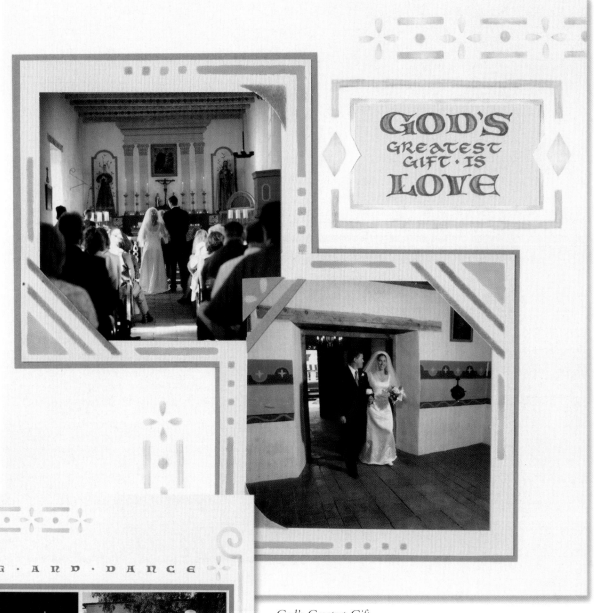

God's Greatest Gift

GOD'S GREATEST GIFT *(above)*

SUPPLIES: various cardstocks, photos, craft knife, stencils, colored pencils, spray adhesive

INSTRUCTIONS

Choose a neutral cardstock for your album page. Double-mat the photos, using two colors of cardstock and a craft knife to cut corner slashes to hold photos. Overlap them on the page. Choose a stencil and pencil colors that echo the Southwestern wedding motifs. Use

The Art of Lettering

Choosing a font or lettering style that reflects your memories and emotions is part of the fun of creating a memory book. Lettering as a graphic design element can strengthen or soften a page, help express poetry or whimsy, or just show your personal style. For lettering inspiration, refer to calligraphy books, type font catalogs, computer font sources, and alphabet books, to name a few.

SUPPLIES: tracing paper, 10-squares-per-inch graph paper, pencil, repositionable tape, soft art eraser, assorted colors of calligraphy pens, gel pens, and colored pencils

INSTRUCTIONS
Plan your lettering on tracing paper on top of your layout page. Choose your phrase, double-checking spelling and details. Roughly lay out the spacing, size, and style of the type you plan to use. Experiment with different pen and pencil types and colors. Test colors on a sample of the actual paper you are using.

Once you have the rough layout on tracing paper, use the graph paper to draw the letters and adjust word spacing. When you are satisfied with your lettering, you're ready to transfer it to the final paper.

If your final paper is transparent, place it directly on top of the graph paper to ink the letters. If your paper is semi-opaque you can use a light box or tape the papers to a bright window and lightly trace the letters in position for inking or coloring.

If you will be transferring the letters to an opaque paper, you can use the pencil-transfer method. Rub soft pencil lead on the backside of the letters you drew on the graph paper. Place the paper pencil side down and use a stylus or inkless pen to transfer a light line as a test. With repositionable tape, place the lettered graph paper over the page in the final position. Use the grid to help align both papers. Trace over the letters, transferring a light image of the words onto the page.

Once you have made the transfer, you are ready to put the final touches on your lettering. Finish the wording with your preferred color and pen or pencil style. If you are using chalk or colored pencils, use spray fixative to prevent undesirable transfer.

When the ink or fixative is dry, lightly erase any visible pencil marks.

the stencil designs to frame the photos and journaling box. Letter a phrase on the cardstock used for the mat, and hand-cut tabs in the neutral cardstock to hold the journaling in place.

MUSICAL MOMENTS *(page 48)*
SUPPLIES: See God's Greatest Gift, page 48

INSTRUCTIONS
Continue the Southwest theme with stencils and colors, but mount the photos in a centered composition and omit the journaling box. Letter directly onto the page.

Elegance in Brocade

A Touch of Victoriana

ELEGANCE IN BROCADE *(above)*

SUPPLIES: various cardstocks, patterned vellum, gold paper, embossing tool and stencil, hole punch, ribbon, photo, photo mounting corners, adhesive

INSTRUCTIONS

Choose a parchment cardstock for the album page. Cut patterned vellum ¼" smaller on all sides than the album page; mount on center of page.

Cut a piece of cardstock 1¾" smaller on all sides than the album page. Place this on a soft surface (such as foam core), and with an embossing tool and stencil, burnish the corner designs into the cardstock. Double-mat the photo and center it on the embossed cardstock. Punch four holes at the top of the photo, as shown above. Thread ribbon through the two middle holes to the back. Cross ribbon behind and bring ribbon back up through middle holes, then thread through side holes to back.

Secure with tape. Add photo mounting corners to the photo mat, and mount to page.

A TOUCH OF VICTORIANA *(above)*

SUPPLIES: cardstock, patterned paper, photos, shape cutters, narrow and wide ribbons, plastic charms or buttons, calligraphy pen and inks, adhesive, tacky glue, page sleeve

INSTRUCTIONS

Use a patterned paper for the album page. Tape wide ribbon in vertical stripes to simulate Victorian wallpaper; glue ribbon ends to the back of the page. Use shape cutters to cut photos, photo mats and journaling box from textured papers. "Hang" the matted photos on the "wallpaper" with narrow ribbon and charms or buttons with tacky glue. If using shank buttons, cut the backs off.

Portrait of a Wedding

PORTRAIT OF A WEDDING *(above)*

SUPPLIES: various cardstocks, photos, tracing paper, vellum, heat-stamp embossing supplies, decorative scissors, gold cord, gold embossed hearts, gold key, adhesive

INSTRUCTIONS

A parchment cardstock was used for the album page. Cut a piece of white cardstock ¾" smaller on all sides than the album page. Use tracing paper to plan the placement and size for your photos and adornments. Trim photos and adhere them to white cardstock using adhesive, leaving a ⅛" border around each. Make journaling boxes from pieces of vellum cut with decorative scissors, and add lettering embossed with a rubber stamp and heat-emboss. Finish with gold accents—cord, hearts, and key.

The World is full of Beauty

When Hearts are full of Love

Hillside Splendor

HILLSIDE SPLENDOR *(above)*

SUPPLIES: cardstock, photos, handmade paper, craft knife, calligraphy pen, adhesive

INSTRUCTIONS

For a natural look choose a rich, earth-toned, colored cardstock for the album page. Tear the edges of a piece of textured handmade paper ¼" smaller on all sides than the page. Scan and enlarge a photo of your wedding location and trim it ¼" smaller on all sides than the hand-made paper. With a craft knife, make small diagonal slices in the corners of the background location photo where the group photo will be centered. Slip the group photo into the sliced corners. Add lettering.

FAMILY, FRIENDS, AND MEMENTOS
(page 53)

SUPPLIES: various cardstocks, photos, handmade paper, memorabilia pocket, spray adhesive

Family, Friends, and Mementos

INSTRUCTIONS

Continuing the colors and theme of Hillside Splendor, arrange two horizontal photos on rectangles of colored cardstock, then position both on a vertical piece of torn handmade paper to unify the images. Preserve and display a memento from the occasion in a memorabilia pocket and mount it at an angle to one side of the photos.

*Banquet in
the Barn*

BANQUET IN THE BARN *(above)*

SUPPLIES: various cardstocks, photos, handmade paper, shape cutters, lettering pen, spray adhesive

INSTRUCTIONS

Crop the photos and mount them on colored cardstock or handmade paper; place at lively angles to reflect the activity of this reception. Use the same papers and the lettering style from the previous pages to continue the theme.

FRIENDS, FOOD, AND FUN *(page 55)*

SUPPLIES: See Banquet in the Barn (left)

INSTRUCTIONS

Use the same techniques as for memory pages on pages 52 and 53.

Best Friends

And Family

Friends, Food, and Fun

DISPLAYING MEMORABILIA

From the engagement party to the honeymoon, you will undoubtedly want to save a variety of wedding memorabilia: small keepsakes, invitations, receipts and other souvenir items. You may also want to keep little organic mementos like small shells, rose petals or colored pebbles, or even whimsical ones like a piece of broken dish or evidence of a spilled glass of wine. You can safely display these pieces in your album by using photo-safe materials when mounting them. Memorabilia pockets come in several sizes (1" square to 4" x 3") and can accommodate trinkets as small as a pinch of sand or rice, or a lock of hair. The larger pockets can store ticket stubs, jewelry, or pressed flowers.

Another method of displaying items such as thank you notes and invitations is to make an envelope to hold the notes. (See Create a Note Card Pocket, page 32.) These envelopes make the mementos easily accessible, without endangering your photos.

A Lovely Veil Frames the Bride

RIBBONS AND LACE IN BLUE *(above)*

SUPPLIES: cardstock, photos, sticker strips, stickers

INSTRUCTIONS

Select blue cardstock for the album page. Make an enlarged color copy of an actual wedding photo, and trim it ½" smaller on all sides than the album page. Mount a smaller photo on the enlarged photo. Use sticker strips and stickers to cover the photo edges and accent the corners.

A LOVELY VEIL FRAMES THE BRIDE *(right)*

SUPPLIES: various cardstocks, patterned vellum, photo, sticker strips, sticker, photo mounting corners, calligraphy pen and ink

INSTRUCTIONS

Cover cardstock with patterned vellum for the album page. Triple-mount the photo on larger rectangles of cardstock, and add colored mounting corners. Use sticker strips to outline the outer blue mat and the mounted journaling box. Letter "love" in colored ink and attach with a sticker. See page 49 for lettering tips.

Tropical Bouquet

TROPICAL BOUQUET *(above)*

SUPPLIES: cardstock, various mulberry papers, photos, shape cutter, decorative-edge scissors, flower punches, alphabet embossing stencil, embossing tool, adhesive

INSTRUCTIONS

Choose a parchment cardstock color for the album page that coordinates with the photos. Use the shape cutter to cut oval photo. Mount the bride's photo on a mulberry paper oval, then soften the edge with decorative-edge scissors. Repeat the decorative-scissor edge on a large square of bright mulberry paper. Enlarge a close-up photo, and mount it toward the upper right corner of the mulberry paper. Mount both images on the cardstock. Use mulberry papers for the flower punches. Scatter them on the page, then use an embossing stencil to inscribe the word "flowers" at the bottom of the page.

Time for Tuxedos

TIME FOR TUXEDOS *(above)*

SUPPLIES: various cardstocks, striped embossed paper, rhinestones, satin ribbon, photos, craft knife, shape cutters, adhesive, tacky glue

INSTRUCTIONS

Choose black cardstock for the album page. Cut striped embossed paper 1" smaller on all sides than page. Make a 1½" cut at the center top of striped embossed paper, and use a large circular template to round the bottom corners. Fold back the sides of the center top cut to create a collar effect. Glue a strip of black ribbon horizontally below the collar points, about 1½" from the top of the shirt. Add a small bow at center. Glue three rhinestones down the front. Use shape cutters to crop the photos and larger double mats of cardstock. Use the green cardstock for the border around the bottom and sides of the shirt.

Cathedral Wedding

CATHEDRAL WEDDING *(above)*

SUPPLIES: various cardstocks, velvet papers, photo, gold embossed embellishments, adhesive, chalk, spray fixative.

INSTRUCTIONS

Use velvet paper for the album page. Double-mount your photo on larger rectangles of gold and velvet papers, and center it on a sheet of black velvet paper in a traditional layout. Mount on gold cardstock. Adhere unit to the album page, and add gold embellishments. For an "antique" look before applying the gold embellishment, reduce the brightness with chalk, and spray them with fixative to seal the chalk dust.

Honeymoon Pop-up Page

PHOTOS FROM YOUR WEDDING CEREMONY or especially your honeymoon will live on stylishly in the form of a clever pop-up. Pop-ups make great gifts, too. We created the fun and eye-catching London Pop-Up using the "scenery flats" technique: use four varied layers of photos plus a background scene. It is important to first make a practice pop-up with cardstock to ensure the display will close correctly and that photos will fit within your card's dimensions when fully folded. ↝

LONDON POP-UP

SUPPLIES: cardstock, heavy cardstock, photos, silver gel pen, gold button, cord, thread

INSTRUCTIONS

The flag of Great Britain cut from red, white, and blue cardstock is the background of this album page. Write names of locations you visited in silver gel pen on the red strips.

Refer to Design a Pop-up on page 61 to construct the card. Cut the letters for "London" out of an enlarged photo and use red cardstock for the year. Keep the pop-up closed with a gold button and cord.

DESIGN A POP-UP

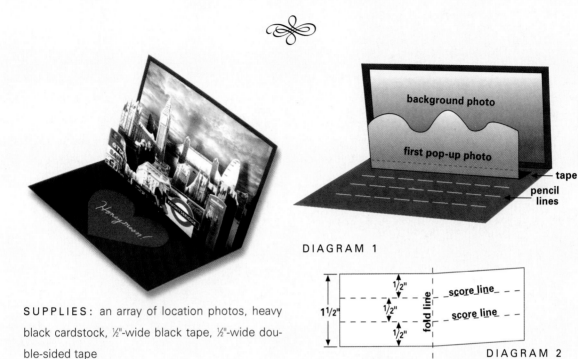

SUPPLIES: an array of location photos, heavy black cardstock, ½"-wide black tape, ½"-wide double-sided tape

INSTRUCTIONS

1. Choose photos with a gradient of distant and close-up images. Scan photos to the scale you want onto heavy photo paper and cut out the scenes as you would like them to appear, leaving the bottom edges straight.

2. Use heavy black cardstock as the base for your card. Score the cardstock in the middle for a horizontal fold. Space your photos at ½" intervals by drawing light pencil lines on the card bottom. Arrange photos so that distant scenes are in the back and close-ups are toward the front. Use ½"-wide black tape to adhere the back bottom edge of the photos to your card along the pencil lines (Diagram 1).

3. To make photo supports, cut 1½"-wide strips of black paper and score them lengthwise at ½" intervals (Diagram 2).

4. Cut the strips about ⅔ of the length of the pho-

tos and fold in half. Tape ½"-wide center areas together with double-sided tape. Clip the folded corners ½" from the top and bottom (Diagram 3).

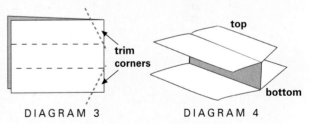

DIAGRAM 3   DIAGRAM 4

5. Fold out four flaps to make an "I-beam" shape (Diagram 4).

6. Use double-sided tape to attach photo supports between photos. Place between photos on their side, taping top and bottom of the "I-beam" flaps to the photos. From the side view, the supports will make an "H" shape and should line up with one another for the pop-up to close properly. From the top view the support placement should be staggered between photos, using 1–2 per photo.

CHOOSING AN ALBUM

Scrapbooks come in many types and sizes. Popular styles, featured in this book, are the strap-hinge and the post-bound types, both of which can expand with refill pages. Pages should number no more than forty to keep your album easy to handle and the binding free from stress. Multiple layers of papers will add considerable weight, in which case you may want to use fewer pages.

Albums come in four basic sizes: 5" x 7", 8½" x 11", 12" x 12", and 12" x 15". In determining which size is best for you, first decide how many photos you have and how many you want to fit on a page. The smallest album can accommodate only one standard snapshot per page and the largest can handle as many as six uncropped photos of the same size, depending on embellishment.

Album Covers

YOUR ALBUM'S COVER IS THE GATEWAY TO your memories, so the first impression you create will set the tone for the pages to follow. You can purchase a ready-made cover and create pages to fit the size, but you can also go one step further and embellish that cover to reflect your own personal style. You can even create your own album from scratch. It's easier than you think!

The best fabrics for album covers are tapestry fabrics, upholstery-weight cotton velvets, brocades, matelasses, and heavy woven wool/polyester blends. To affix these fabrics, spread a very thin but uniform layer of adhesive over the surface. To ensure that your corners and inside folds stay affixed, use a heavier and evenly spread application of the glue, but be careful not to let it soak through the fabric. This seepage will not dry invisibly, and you will be left with an undesirable darker spot in the fabric. ❧

WHITE LACE ALBUM *(page 62)*
SUPPLIES: purchased square album, square lace handkerchief, cardstock, matte medium (a fixative), foam core board, craft knife, velvet paper, tacky glue, satin piping, rice paper, string of faux pearls, flower punches, individual faux pearls, ribbon

INSTRUCTIONS
1. See Choosing an Album, page 62. Choose a lace handkerchief that fits or is slightly smaller than the front of the album cover. Apply a smooth layer of matte medium to the album cover and position the lace handkerchief on top. When dry, apply a second coat of matte medium to the top to prevent it from slipping.
2. Cut a piece of foam core board 2" smaller on all sides than the cover. Cut velvet paper 1" larger on all sides than the foam core, center over the foam core, and glue. Fold edges of velvet paper to the back of the foam core and glue, referring to Diagram 1 of Hand-Made Accordion Albums on page 68 to trim corners.

3. Use tacky glue to attach satin piping around sides of velvet paper assembly. Center unit over lace handkerchief and glue to album.
4. Tear edges of rice paper carefully so they are 1" smaller on all sides than the velvet unit; center rice paper on top of velvet unit. Secure it in place with matte medium.
5. Cut another square of foam core about ¾" smaller than the velvet square. In the exact center of this square, draw a 1¾" square. Using a craft knife, cut a window out of the center of the foam core.
6. Cover the entire piece of foam core with another square of velvet paper ½" larger on all sides than the foam core. Glue velvet paper to the foam core. Turn over, and draw an X on the inside window diagonally from corner to corner. With a craft knife, slash on the X lines; turn and glue slashed points to back of foam core (see diagram page 64). Center and glue wrapped window assembly to top of album cover. Glue a string of pearls around this square.
7. Refer to Punched Flowers on page 43. Fill the window opening with 36 double flower punches and small pearls with tacky glue to add varied textures and dimensions.

TIED WITH LOVE ALBUM *(page 64)*
SUPPLIES: purchased square album, foam core board, handmade paper, adhesive, craft knife, linen or cotton fabric to match album, cardstock, mulberry paper, patterned paper, plastic rings, dove stickers, narrow silk ribbon, tacky glue

INSTRUCTIONS
1. See Choosing an Album, page 62.
2. To make the ring assembly page for the "peek-a-boo" album cover, first cut a sheet of neutral-colored cardstock ½" smaller on all sides than the album cover. Tear the edges of mulberry paper 2" smaller on all sides than the cardstock; tear the handmade paper 1¾" smaller on

Tied with Love Album (top cover)

Tied with Love Album
(peek-a-boo page)

all sides than the mulberry paper. Cut a piece of patterned paper ¾" smaller on all sides than the handmade paper. Layer and center these four papers on top of each other, graduating from the largest to the smallest on top. Adhere with adhesive to fix them in position.

3. Tie the rings together with a ribbon bow. Center on the patterned paper square and glue under the knot of the bow. Gracefully attach the ends of the ribbon with dove stickers. Cut the banner freehand and hand-letter the names.

4. Create the "over-cover" for the rings to peek through by following steps 1–2 of A Scattering of Pansies Album on page 69, except wrap the handmade paper over all four edges of foam core and glue to inside. Be sure your opening is ¼" smaller on all sides than the edges of the top patterned paper square below the rings. Position the over-cover next to the left edge of the album cover (right).

5. Cut a strip of linen or cotton fabric 3" wide and 1" longer than the height of your album. Turn the short edges under ½". Center the strip over the right edge of the back side of the foam core over-cover and the left side of the album cover, then glue.

6. Finish the inside of the over-cover by cutting a sheet of coordinating cardstock ⅛" smaller on all sides than the album cover. Glue to the inside left cover to hide wrapped edges and fabric edges.

7. Attach the layered ring assembly page to the cover and add photo mounting corners.

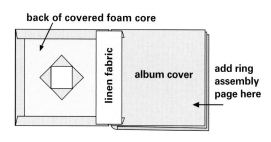

back of covered foam core

linen fabric

album cover

add ring
assembly
page here

Vintage Memento Album (below)
Portrait in Perfection Album (right)

VINTAGE MEMENTO ALBUM *(above left)*

SUPPLIES: small purchased album, fabric, cardstock, spray adhesive or glue stick, tacky glue, wide ribbon, jewelry accents, wire cutters

INSTRUCTIONS

See Choosing an Album, page 62. Using spray adhesive or a glue stick, cover your purchased album in fabric. Cut 2" larger than album. Fold edges to back and glue down (see Diagram 1, page 68) to trim corners. Choose the jewelry you wish to use and cut off any clasps with wire cutters. Position ribbon diagonally and glue to album cover, turning ends to back. Position and glue jewelry on ribbon with tacky glue.

For a smooth, clean look for the inside of your album cover, cut a matching sheet of cardstock, and adhere hiding the raw edges of the fabric.

PORTRAIT IN PERFECTION ALBUM
(above right)

SUPPLIES: large purchased album, fabrics, cardstock, spray adhesive or glue stick, tacky glue, ribbon, pre-cut photo mats, photo, photo sleeve, jewelry accent, wire cutters

INSTRUCTIONS

See Choosing an Album, page 62. Using the same technique as for the Vintage Memento Album (left), cover a 12" x 12" keepsake book with coordinating fabric and ribbon. Create the photo frame by covering a pre-cut mat with fabric. Position a gold mat inside the frame. Insert your photo in a photo sleeve and insert it in the mat. Offset the photo assembly and glue it to the cover, adding the jewelry accent last.

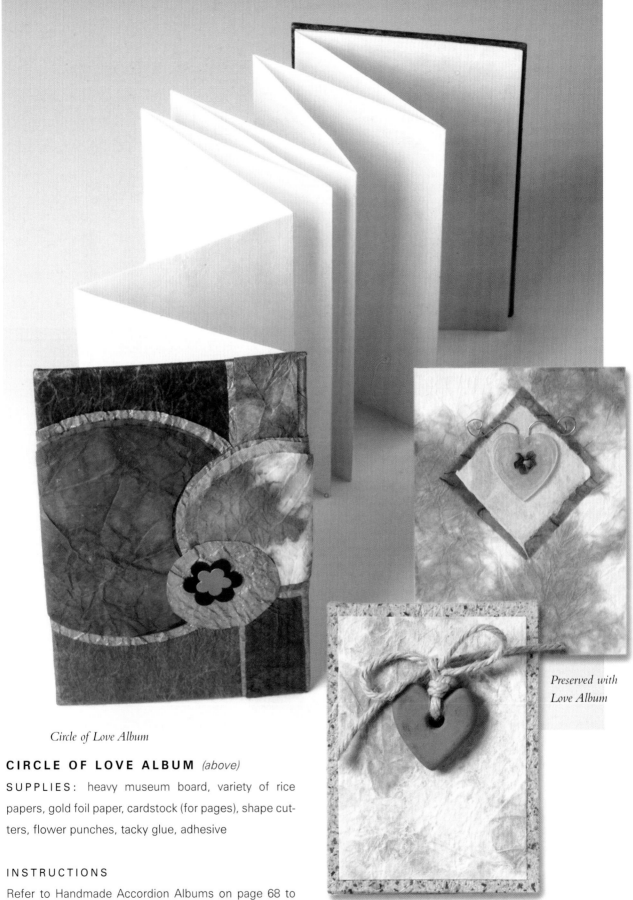

Circle of Love Album

CIRCLE OF LOVE ALBUM *(above)*

SUPPLIES: heavy museum board, variety of rice papers, gold foil paper, cardstock (for pages), shape cutters, flower punches, tacky glue, adhesive

INSTRUCTIONS

Refer to Handmade Accordion Albums on page 68 to make a basic accordion album covered with rice paper.

Preserved with
Love Album

Memories Held by Heart Album

Joyful Memories Album

Embellish the front cover with handmade and gold foil papers cut into a variety of circular shapes that complement the rectangles. This composition uses elements of shape and scale (see Designing Your Pages, page 27). Carry the design into the book by wrapping the large circle around the cover and attaching it to the first page. Flower punches add a finishing focal counterpoint to the geometric shapes.

PRESERVED WITH LOVE ALBUM *(page 66)*

SUPPLIES: heavy museum board, handmade paper, rice paper, mulberry paper, cardstock (for pages), plastic heart charm, wire, tacky glue, adhesive

INSTRUCTIONS

Refer to Handmade Accordion Albums on page 68 to make a basic accordion album covered with rice paper. Tear rice and mulberry papers into squares. Rotate them to form a diamond shape and adhere. Finish with a decorative heart charm and wire accents glued in place.

MEMORIES HELD BY HEART ALBUM
(page 66)

SUPPLIES: heavy museum board, handmade papers, cardstock (for pages), twine, terra cotta heart, foam spacers

INSTRUCTIONS

Refer to Handmade Accordion Albums on page 68 to make a basic accordion album covered with handmade papers. For a natural look, choose papers that coordinate with the natural fibers of the twine and terra cotta heart. Use foam spacers to mount the heart.

JOYFUL MEMORIES ALBUM *(above)*

SUPPLIES: purchased album, handmade paper, greeting card, decorative scissors, tacky glue, ribbon

INSTRUCTIONS

See Choosing an Album, page 62. Select an attractive congratulatory card and mount the card onto two layers of handmade paper in bright colors. Glue the assemblage to the album cover and add a shiny, ribbon bow.

HAND-MADE ACCORDION ALBUMS

SUPPLIES: medium- to heavy-weight museum board, decorative paper for cover, embellishments, large piece of paper (22" x 30") for inside pages (cardstock, rice paper, drawing paper, or watercolor paper), tacky glue

INSTRUCTIONS

1. To make covers: cut two pieces of museum board the size you want your album to be.

2. Make a tracing paper pattern for the paper cover by adding ¾" to all sides of museum board. Use pattern to cut out two pieces of decorative paper.

3. Brush glue onto the surface of the museum board. Smooth the decorative paper down on the board. Trim corners (Diagram 1).

4. On the back of the board, brush glue onto the flaps of the paper and carefully turn in the sides to form a smooth corner. Repeat for the back album cover.

5. To make inside pages: use the longer side of the large paper. Cut a strip ½" shorter than the height of

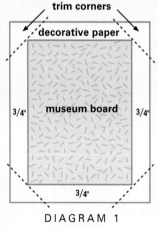

DIAGRAM 1

the cover. Folded pages should be ½" narrower than the width of the cover. To be able to open the album from either side, as you would a book, be sure you have an even number of folded pages (Diagram 2).

HINT: To cut the proper length of paper, make a pattern on scrap paper first, making sure that all of your folded pages are the same size so that the last piece is perfectly fitted when you glue it to the back cover.

6. To create folded pages, measure the width of the cover less ½" and make the first fold. Continue to fold accordion style, trimming off the last page when you are finished, so all pages are even.

7. To create more pages, add another strip by folding over a ½" edge on the new strip and gluing the new section to the previous strip. Continue to fold as in first strip.

8. To finish the album, glue the pages at either end to the front and back inside covers, centering on cover to leave ¼" edge of album cover showing on all four sides.

9. Embellish the album with more decorative paper, photos, charms or ribbons to create a unique memory book that is beautifully crafted and worthy of housing your prized wedding mementos.

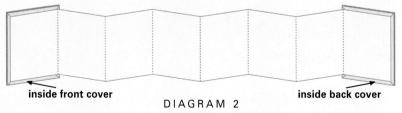

inside front cover   inside back cover

DIAGRAM 2

A Scattering of Pansies Album

A SCATTERING OF PANSIES ALBUM

(above)

SUPPLIES: purchased album, foam core board, handmade paper, cardstock, tacky glue, craft knife, matte medium, ribbon, pressed dried flowers, photo, adhesive

INSTRUCTIONS

1. See Choosing an Album, page 62. Cut foam core the same size as the album cover.

2. With the craft knife, cut a window in the center of the foam core the same size as your photo. Cut handmade paper 1½" larger than the foam core on all sides and use tacky glue to adhere it to the top of the foam core. Turn the paper edge under on the edge along the spine and glue. DO NOT glue the remaining outside edges. Carefully slash the window in an X-shape from corner to corner. Wrap the paper edges around the foam core to the inside of the window and glue to back of foam core (see diagram on page 64).

3. Choose a cardstock that compliments the original album cover's color or pattern and cut it the same size as the foam core. Crop your photo ⅛" smaller on all sides than the finished size of the window. Affix the photo on the mat paper so that it can be framed by the cutout and show an ⅛" border. Adhere the matted photo in position on the back of the foam core.

4. Glue the foam core board to the top of the album cover. Wrap the handmade paper over the remaining three edges of the album cover and glue to the inside.

5. Arrange pressed dried flowers around window and glue in position, using matte medium or matte varnish. Tie a ribbon around the album cover (see photo) and glue the ends to the inside.

6. To finish the inside of the cover, cut a sheet of matching paper or coordinating cardstock ⅛" smaller on all sides than the album cover. Glue to inside cover to hide wrapped edges.

7. If you desire, cover the spine and back cover to match.

Mardi Gras Glitter Shadow Box

Displays of Affection

PRECIOUS WEDDING PICTURES AND mementos lend themselves beautifully to artful displays you can enjoy every day. Arranging a lively collage of memorabilia for a shadow box allows you to show off three-dimensional items that don't fit in an album. Your best photos will look even better framed and surrounded by romantic stickers and pressed flowers from your bouquet. A storage box tells the tale of your honeymoon trip and also holds treasures within. Let the fun continue! ❧

MARDI GRAS GLITTER SHADOW BOX
(page 70)

SUPPLIES: shadow box, cardstock, invitation, photos, photo sleeves, tacky glue, photo mounting corners, memorabilia, foam spacers, sticker letters, stickers, bubble bottle favor, *Mardi Gras* beads

INSTRUCTIONS

Remove back of shadow box and cut a background of black cardstock. Trim and curl the party invitation at the ends like a scroll. Insert photos in photo sleeves with photo mounting corners. Affix other souvenirs and memorabilia with foam spacers to create a variety of depths. Glue a champagne bubble bottle favor to the inside of the shadow box. Add star stickers scattered throughout. Spell out *L'aissez les bon temps roulez!* ("Let the good time roll" in French) using gold foil sticker letters on the box's glass front. Finish with festive *Mardi Gras* beads on the outside of the box, and fix them in position on the back with glue.

KEEPSAKES FOREVER SHADOW BOX
(left)

SUPPLIES: shadow box, foam core board, embossed textured paper, pre-cut embossed mat, photo, invitation, memorabilia, glue dots, foam tape or small pins, tacky glue

INSTRUCTIONS

Adhere a piece of embossed, textured paper with tacky glue to foam core board that fits the shadow box's frame. Insert the photo into a pre-cut mat and place near the center of the composition. Assemble the memorabilia to encircle the photo, layering the various items according to their visual or sentimental interest. Once you are happy with the composition, use glue dots, foam tape or small pins push into the foam core board at an angle to hold the items in place.

Keepsakes Forever Shadow Box

Dreams Come True Box offers two ways to keep your memories alive: ample surface to display travel memorabilia and maps from your honeymoon, and an interior storage area for other wedding memorabilia.

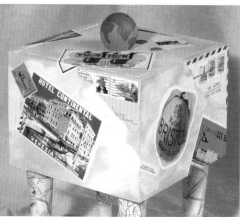

DREAMS COME TRUE BOX *(page 72)*

SUPPLIES: wooden storage box (8" square x 6" high), gesso, acrylic paint, matte medium, memorabilia, map pages, wooden ball, 5" furniture legs with feet, screws, drill

INSTRUCTIONS

Assemble, gesso (if necessary), and paint the box with a sky motif. Paint furniture legs to match, then attach them to the bottom of the box with screws. To create a handle, paint a map of the earth on a wooden ball and attach it to the top from the inside with a screw. Use matte medium to add honeymoon memorabilia such as brushed-on stamps, letters, postcards, stickers, and for-eign coins. Glue map pages cut to size onto the legs. Use matte medium to seal the entire box.

WEDDING POTPOURRI FRAME *(below)*

SUPPLIES: frame, handmade paper, patterned paper, cardstock, photos, pressed dried flowers, matte medium, stickers

INSTRUCTIONS

Double-mount the photos on cardstock and patterned paper, then arrange on a handmade paper background. Add dried pressed flowers with matte medium and then add stickers. Mount the assemblage in a frame to enjoy for years to come.

Wedding Potpourri Frame

Handmade Paper

PAPER RECEIVES AND PRESERVES OUR SECRETS, DOCUMENTS solemn events and joyous occasions, and announces our glad tidings to the world. We share our finest times with paper. If only we could put more into paper than words….

What if you could capture the fragrance of your wedding bouquet in paper, or convey the sheen of your silken gown to a friend far away? What if a page could recall again the ruby glow of wine and the warmth of wedding wishes?

All things are possible. All these things are hidden in paper—these things and more, if you put them there. With your own hands, smooth the scattered bits and tendrils of your wedding day into sheets of thick, memorable paper, garden-scented and tinted with dawn.

Tease threads from scraps of silk and tulle, gather stray petals dropped by giddy flowers, borrow the silvery shine of ribbon curls and the glitter of the evening. Blend these things with the subtle fibers of trees and leaves, and paper is at your fingertips, waiting to blush with radiant rosé or shy, golden tea.

And what can you do with such rare paper? What can you not do with a paper made from joy? Such wondrous paper awaits sonnets, or whispers under an anniversary pillow. Such paper graces the writing desks of ladies until it bears messages of love and hope hidden in its folds. Such paper is full of secrets and shares them gladly.

PAPERMAKING

Chapter designed and written by Ellaraine Lockie

A wonderful way of commemorating a wedding is to incorporate items from the occasion into beautiful sheets of handmade paper. The resulting stationery, greeting cards, and artwork make lovely souvenirs for the wedded couple and their families. Materials which can successfully be used for handmade paper abound at wedding and wedding-related events. Gather these items yourself or enlist a crew to help you collect them during pre-wedding festivities such as showers, engagement parties, bachelor/bachelorette parties, and rehearsal dinners.

Make your paper pulp using leftover invitations, programs, menus, and other paper products. Color it with napkins or certain flowers and foliage from the ceremony or reception. (Coffee or tea from the reception actually makes a good natural paper dye.) Embedding wedding-related items in handmade paper gives it color and texture and serves to preserve small bits and pieces of mementos in an artistic way. Consider incorporating into your paper flowers and foliage, glitter and confetti, wrapping paper, ribbon, and tidbits of leftover lace and tulle from bridal attire, as well as components from table centerpieces, favors, and more.

PAPERMAKING EQUIPMENT AND SUPPLIES

There are many resources to help you get started. You will find a list of papermaking supply companies on page 94 (see Resources); most of these companies have catalogs and will supply products by mail order.

Always use stainless steel, glass, wood, or unchipped enamel equipment for papermaking. Never use aluminum, tin, or iron because they may create unattractive brown spots on the paper. Your papermaking pots and utensils should be different from the ones you use for food preparation. Store them separately as well.

The following is a list of general equipment and supplies you will want to have available.

❧ Recycled invitations, programs, menus, napkins, and other paper products; use high quality paper products for making pulp.

❧ Abaca fiber from the leafstalk of a type of banana tree is often used as the basis for handmade paper. You can purchase partially processed abaca fiber in sheets from papermaking suppliers.

❧ Mold and deckle: Purchase a mold and deckle from a papermaking supply company (see Resources) or follow directions on page 78 to make your own. The plastic vat (listed below) should be at least 7" deep, with an area large enough for your mold and deckle to easily fit inside.

❧ Blender
❧ Plastic vat or tub
❧ Measuring cups and spoons
❧ Medium-sized bowl
❧ Toothbrush, meat baster, all-purpose brush
❧ Stainless steel pots
❧ Scissors, knife, single-edged razor blade
❧ High quality, absorbent sponge
❧ Strainer
❧ Spray bottle
❧ Large acrylic boards, at least ¼" thick
❧ Thick absorbent towels
❧ Wooden spoons
❧ Five-gallon bucket
❧ Liquid starch (see page 79)

Equipment and supplies (from upper left): blender (1), vat and towels (2), measuring cups (3), glass bowl (4), meat baster, all-purpose brush, toothbrush (5), stainless steel pots (6), scissors, knife (7), sponge (8), strainer (9), spray bottle (10), acrylic boards (11), wooden spoons, paper towels (12)

MAKING A MOLD AND DECKLE

A mold is a frame with an attached screen that you use to form a sheet of paper. A deckle is a frame exactly the same size as the mold (minus the screen) that you place on top of the mold to prevent the fiber from running off. The deckle produces handmade paper's characteristic deckled edges. Look for brass strainer screen at a plumbing or hardware store, but do not use screen door screen.

SUPPLIES: wooden stretcher bars from an art supply store (or ¾" plywood and waterproof glue and sandpaper) waterproofing sealant, brass strainer screen with 30 or 40 mesh, kitchen shears, staple gun and staples, duct tape

INSTRUCTIONS

1. Use waterproof glue to assemble wooden stretcher bars into two frames. The space inside the frames determines the size of your paper. Alternately, you can make stronger frames from plywood. The wooden edges should be about 1" wide. Sand the edges lightly, waterproof them with a sealant, and let dry.

2. With kitchen shears, cut a piece of brass strainer screen about 2" larger than the space inside the frames. Wear gloves to protect yourself from the sharp edges. Use a staple gun to attach the screen to one of the frames. Start by putting one staple in the center of the north side, then ask a helper to pull tightly on the screen while you place a second staple in the center of the south side. Next, put one staple in the center of the east side of the frame. Then, have your assistant pull tightly on the screen while you put the next staple in the center of the west side. Now, place staples about every 2" all around the screen, alternating sides with each staple and having your helper pull tightly on the screen each time. It is important to have a very tightly-stretched screen.

3. Cover the wood on the screen side with duct tape. Over time, the screen may start to sag. You can then simply replace the duct tape and screen instead of making a brand new mold and deckle.

Leftover wedding invitations and programs make excellent pulp for handmade paper.

MAKING THE PULP

Leftover wedding invitations, programs, menus, and other high quality paper products make excellent pulp for your handmade paper. Using high-quality paper products give your sheets strength. To create truly beautiful paper, always use some abaca in the pulp (see Resources). Abaca makes sheet-forming easier, which results in thinner yet stronger papers. The recommended ratio of abaca to recycled paper is 50:50. If high-quality leftover paper isn't available, you can use 100 percent abaca for the pulp.

SUPPLIES: ⅓ lb. paper to recycle (invitations, programs, menus, etc.), ⅓ lb. partially processed abaca fiber, blender, strainer, medium-sized bowl, five-gallon bucket, liquid starch (commercial or homemade, see Step 5)

INSTRUCTIONS

1. Soak about ⅓ lb. abaca in a large bowl of water for at least 30 minutes. Tear it into 1" pieces. (This will make about 40 sheets of thin paper.)

2. Soak leftover papers in a large bowl of water for at least 30 minutes, then tear them into 1" pieces.

3. Place a handful of torn abaca pieces (¼ to ⅓ cup) into a blender and fill two-thirds with water. Run the blender on high speed for about 30 seconds. Add a handful (¼ to ⅓ cup) of torn leftover paper. Run the blender for another 30 seconds. Precise timing is not critical; it is important to run the blender long enough to macerate the fibers evenly, but not so long that you weaken them. If you use 100 percent abaca for the pulp, run the blender for about one minute, total. If you use 100 percent recycled papers, run the blender for about 30 seconds.

4. To test for consistency, place a teaspoon of the pulp into a jar of water, cover and shake. The fibers should reduce to an even fineness. If lumps remain, blend the mixture longer. Pour the blended pulp into a large bucket and repeat steps one through three until smooth.

5. Size the pulp to make it water-resistant by stirring in two to three cups of concentrated commercial liquid starch or four cups of homemade liquid starch. Starch makes the paper water-repellent and bleed-resistant so that you can write on it. To make enough liquid starch for a five-gallon bucket of well-sized pulp (enough for 60–70 sheets of paper), stir ¼ cup cornstarch into ¼ cup cold water until dissolved. Bring 3¾ cups water to a boil.

FORMING THE SHEETS

1. Plunge the mold/deckle, submarine-style, toward the bottom of the vat.

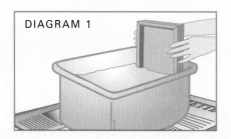

DIAGRAM 1

2. Once it's completely submerged, level the mold/deckle into a horizontal position.

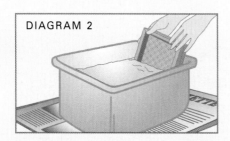

DIAGRAM 2

3. Keeping the mold/deckle horizontal, bring it slowly to the surface. A thin layer of fiber will remain on the screen.

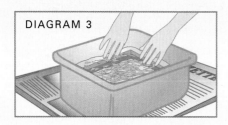

DIAGRAM 3

4. Give the mold and deckle four quick little shakes. Drain off excess water.

DIAGRAM 4

Gradually add the cornstarch mixture while stirring. Simmer and continue stirring for two minutes until the mixture is lump-free. Use immediately, or reheat to the boiling point right before using. Let the pulp set for at least 30 minutes before forming the sheets. This amount of sizing is appropriate for stationery; papers intended for other purposes may need less or no sizing at all.

FORMING THE SHEETS

SUPPLIES: vat, acrylic boards, spray bottle

INSTRUCTIONS

When forming your sheets of paper, first place newspapers around the vat to soak up any dripping water. Fill the vat about two-thirds full of water and add eight to ten cups of pulp. The proportion of pulp to water determines the thickness of a sheet: the more pulp, the thicker your paper. Use more pulp if you haven't used part abaca to make the pulp. Each time you form a new sheet, add another one to two cups of pulp to the vat. Once you determine your paper's desired thickness, add the appropriate amount of pulp before forming each sheet. This will ensure uniform sheets.

Next, wet the mold's screen by dipping it into the vat. Position the mold, screen-side up, in one hand and place the deckle over the top of the mold. With your other hand and fingers spread wide, stir the pulp vigorously in the vat, in a lengthwise direction only, until the pulp is well dispersed. (Stirring in a lengthwise direction only, helps to avoid splashing water out of the vat.) This will take 15–20 seconds the first time, but only a few seconds with each subsequent sheet. If you stop making sheets for any length of time, however, stir the vat water again for 15–20 seconds before making the next sheet. Stirring

ELECTRICAL SAFETY: Keep your work area as dry as possible, and install ground-fault circuit interrupters on outlets near sinks and blender areas.

keeps the pulp from settling on the bottom of the vat. Pulp fibers must be well dispersed or the paper will be thick in some areas and thin in others.

Hold the mold and deckle in both hands, and plunge them, submarine-style, toward the bottom of the vat (Diagram 1, page 80). The leading edge should be almost vertical when entering the water, before you level the mold and deckle into a horizontal position once it's completely submerged (Diagram 2, page 80). Keeping the mold/deckle horizontal, bring it slowly to the surface again. A thin layer of wet fibers will remain on the screen (Diagram 3, page 80). Give the mold and deckle four quick little shakes. Make each shake a quick tilt—just one to two inches in each direction—from side to side lengthwise, and from side to side widthwise. Do not tilt any more than this, and do not tilt slowly because the fiber may slide on the screen. These shakes are important because they make the wet fibers interlock in all directions to form strong sheets of paper. Drain the excess water (Diagram 4, page 80).

When most of the water has drained, rest the mold and deckle on the edge of the vat with one hand (Diagram 5, right). Remove the deckle with your other hand. When removing the deckle, lift it straight up from the mold, vertically, keeping it absolutely level while moving it across the mold. This movement is important so that water does not drip from the deckle leaving visible water spots on the dried paper. If at any time you want to throw a wet sheet back into the vat water and start over, just place the mold, screen-side down on the water's surface; the pulp on the screen will release into the vat. Stir the vat of pulp water again (in a lengthwise direc-

CLEAN UP: Paper pulp can clog your drain, so strain the pulp out of the water before disposing of the water. Scrub the mold's screen with a toothbrush and running water after use, so that dried pulp will not clog the holes.

5. Lay frame on side of vat; remove deckle.

6. Lay mold (fiber side up) on a stack of newspapers and gently blot with a towel.

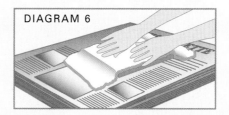

7. Flip the mold onto an acrylic board sprayed with water.

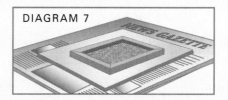

8. Sponge water out of the sheet, pressing it against the back of the screen and squeezing water out of the sponge into a bowl.

9. Remove mold from the board, leaving the paper sheet.

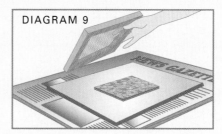

Beautiful deckled edges add to the charm of handmade paper sheets.

tion) for just a few seconds, to disperse the fibers before starting over.

Take the mold off the edge of the vat and place it on a stack of newspapers, fiber side up. Fold a thick towel in half, gently place it over the fiber on the screen and lightly press along its surface (Diagram 6, page 81). Do not drag the towel across the fibers or press too hard; the idea is to press just enough water out of the fiber so that it is strong enough to come off the mold successfully. The more water you remove from the fiber, the stronger it becomes. Do not towel-blot more than once, however. If you remove too much water at this stage, the paper sheet will dry too quickly when laid on the acrylic board, causing the sheet's edges to crinkle.

Lastly, liberally spray a section of the acrylic board the size of your paper with water from a spray bottle. The acrylic board must be wet so the paper can dry without crinkling (Diagram 7, page 81). Flip the mold onto the wet acrylic, fiber side down. Sponge water out of the sheet by firmly pressing a sponge against the back of the screen, squeezing the water out of the sponge into a bowl as you work (Diagram 8, page 81). Go over all areas of the sheet with the sponge four or five times. Remove the mold from the board by lifting it from one of its shorter ends, leaving the sheet of fiber on the board (Diagram 9, page 81). Gently press the sheet with the sponge another couple of times, removing more water and pressing out any remaining air bubbles.

DRYING THE SHEETS

To dry the handmade paper sheets you have just formed, leave the sheets on the acrylic board indoors, out of sunlight and away from drafts, until they are thoroughly dry. This will take one to two days, depending on the thickness of the paper, the humidity, and the temperature. The sheets must dry slowly so they do not crinkle or warp. Slow drying also allows the fibers to shrink naturally, giving the paper greater folding strength.

Once the paper is completely dry, carefully peel it from the acrylic board, starting at two corners. If the edges stick, use a single-edged razor blade to carefully loosen them. The paper should feel crisp after you remove it. If it feels limp, finish drying it between paper towels with a heavy book or similar weight on top. If the dry papers curl, stack them together and place a weight on top for a few hours to flatten.

COLORING THE PAPER

There are many ways to color handmade paper. General directions for natural and commercial dyeing are available in numerous basic papermaking instruction books. It is easy to dye your handmade paper using colored program covers, menus or invitations in your pulp. You can also use wedding-related items such as solid colored paper napkins, certain flowers, leaves and stems, and even leftover reception coffee and tea. If using organic products, a mordant will help fix the colors.

Some people may be allergic to alum. Keep mordant pulp with alum away from food or food preparation areas and wear a dust mask during use.

Recycled program covers give these sheets an attractive rosy color.

MORDANT

A mordant is a substance that allows the dye color to be fixed to the pulp. Without it, the color will remain in the water. Some mordants are extremely toxic, however. One of the safest mordants is alum in the form of ammonium aluminum sulfate, used in home pickling and available at drug stores. Alum in the form of aluminum acetate works slightly better and produces stronger colors. This alum is available through dye suppliers. Caution: always wear a dust mask when preparing alum.

To make the mordant, dissolve ½ cup alum into one pint of hot water. Stir the mixture into a large, stainless steel cooking pot containing strained pulp. Soak the pulp for a few hours or overnight.

COLORING WITH PAPER NAPKINS

Solid colored paper napkins from a variety of your wedding events provide a fast and easy method for coloring the pulp.

INSTRUCTIONS

1. Soak the napkins in water for several minutes.
2. Tear the wet napkins into 1" pieces. Place the pieces

from one napkin into the blender with the abaca/recycled papers and blend as usual. If you want a lighter, pastel shade, use fewer colored napkin pieces in each blender load. If you want brighter color, use a greater number of pieces.

COLORING WITH FLOWERS, LEAVES AND STEMS

Certain flowers, leaves, and stems, such as sunflowers, marigolds, yellow cosmos, and black-eyed Susans, are sources of natural dyes. You can find listings of those appropriate for dyeing in books that teach basic natural dyeing, or you can try soaking wedding flowers, leaves, and stems in hot water to see if any color exudes into the liquid. If so, the materials are most likely suitable for dyeing paper pulp.

INSTRUCTIONS

1. Follow directions for preparing the mordant (left).
2. Place the flowers/leaves/stems into a large cooking pot and cover with water. Bring to a boil and simmer until color bleeds from the raw materials (about an hour). Strain and discard the flowers/leaves/stems and set the water aside.
3. Rinse the pulp well and strain. Return the pulp to the cooking pot.

Napkins from the engagement party and showers provide the color for these handmade sheets.

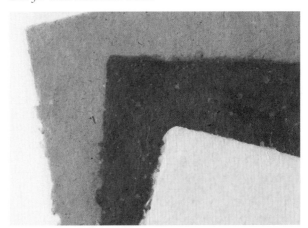

Color your paper with natural dye from sunflowers to create a sheet with a subtle green hue (top) or use coffee to dye the pulp for an attractive earthtoned envelope (bottom).

4. Add your reserved colored water to the pulp and heat to just below boiling. Turn off the heat; leave for several hours or overnight.

5. Strain and run the pulp briefly through the blender process again. Continue papermaking.

COLORING WITH COFFEE AND TEA INSTRUCTIONS

1. Follow directions for preparing the mordant, page 83.

2. Rinse the pulp in a strainer.

3. Pour strong, blended coffee or tea over the pulp and heat to just below boiling point. Turn off heat and leave for several hours or overnight. Continue papermaking.

SCENTING THE PAPER

Scented papers made from essential or perfumed oils are lovely gifts for others as well as charming keepsakes for yourself. You can often match oils with flowers used in your wedding festivities, such as rose, geranium, carnation, lilac, lavender and violet; you can also match greenery such as pine and fir for December weddings. Match colors, too, using orange essential oil for orange and rust colored papers, lemon oil for yellows and golds, and lime oils for green shades.

Laminate wedding flowers, ferns, ivy, and other foliage between two sheets of paper to get a beautiful translucent effect.

To create a notable scent, add a few drops of essential or perfumed oil to the pulp or to the vat before making the sheets. This method scents your entire working area while you are making the paper.

If you prefer to add just a hint of fragrance, add the scent to the papers after they have completely dried. Soak a cotton ball in several drops of essential or perfumed oil. Then wrap the scented ball in a facial tissue (so it doesn't stain the papers), and place the ball in a box large enough to hold the papers. Place the papers in the box and cover. They'll be ready after several days—or you can store them this way indefinitely. They will retain a subtle but distinct scent.

LAMINATING

There are many clever ways to showcase your wedding mementos. One method is lamination—pressing two pieces of wet, handmade paper together until they fuse into one piece. Almost any flat, lightweight material can be sandwiched between two sheets of wet paper, creating a see-through effect. Try using feathers, leaves, pressed petals, and even decorated tissue paper from shower, engagement and wedding gifts.

INSTRUCTIONS

1. Use white or cream-colored pulp. Make thin sheets that retain a translucent quality when the paper is dry. Sponge the first sheet of paper on the acrylic drying board, then place the material you want to sandwich on top of the wet sheet, and place the second sheet on top.
2. To keep this paper layer very thin, do not add any pulp to the vat for the top sheet. Position the mold with the top sheet on it so that it exactly covers the sheet of paper on the acrylic board. Sponge in the usual manner. You can line up the sheets by marking the acrylic board so that you know where to place the mold each time. Finish the sheets in the usual way, but be aware that these sheets will take longer to dry than your single sheets.

Papers with embedded mementos hold special meaning for the newlyweds: program papers (top); fresh flower petals (second and third from top); cut-up centerpiece foil and dried petals (bottom).

EMBEDDING WEDDING MEMENTOS IN PAPER

A good scavenger eye at wedding events results in future fun–making embedded papers with your finds. Use the following embedding methods in conjunction with one another to achieve varied textures.

NOTE: Embedded papers take up to twice as long to dry as single sheet, unadorned papers.

BLENDER METHOD

If you want texture but require a relatively smooth surface for writing, add small bits of material in the final few seconds of blending the pulp. Some additives are fragile and require only one short push on the blender button;

others require two to three seconds of blending. For paper intended for stationery, pre-soak the bits you want to add to the blender until they are saturated so they hydrate and are less likely to float to the top of the pulp.

This technique works well with additives like flower petals, leaves, foliage, moss, glitter, or pieces of paper. Tear or cut these items to no larger than 1" in size.

PULP BUCKET METHOD

If you want items to keep their shapes in your paper, add small amounts of these items to your pulp bucket after the pulp has been blended, and stir well. You can use wedding mementos too fragile to go in the blender or those you don't want to chop into pieces, such as whole leaves, flowers, feathers, bits of lace, threads, or confetti. This technique is especially good for text you have cut out from programs and invitations.

VAT METHOD

If you want a rugged texture on one side and smooth on the other, add small bits of material to the vat before stirring it to form the sheets. You can use the same types of materials as for the blender and pulp methods.

The materials tend to float to the surface, so most of the added pieces will appear on the side that dries against the board, creating a rough texture.

MEAT BASTER METHOD

Use a meat baster to embed delicate or lightweight items, such as pressed flowers, exactly where you want them.

Sponge the sheet on the acrylic board, then place the item you wish to embed on top of the sheet. Fill a meat baster with pulp water from the vat. Hold the baster about ½" above the surface of the item and dribble the pulp all around the item's edge, avoiding direct contact with the item or the paper. Lightly sponge off excess water. You may need to repeat this procedure or drip vat water across the entire item, depending on the weight and size of the object and how easily it embeds.

Examples of embedding materials using various methods: fresh flowers embedded by vat method (top); wedding ribbons embedded by vat method, words embedded by meat baster method (second from top); dried flower petals and foil from centerpiece embedded by pulp method (third from top); program strings embedded by blender method (bottom).

Examples using pulp and vat methods of embedding: wedding ribbons by vat method (top); confetti and veil tulle by pulp and vat methods (second from top); veil tulle, confetti and ribbon by pulp and vat methods; ring favors embedded by meat baster method (bottom).

Examples using pulp bucket method of embedding: confetti from Christmas wedding (top); invitation paper pieces (second from top); dried wedding flower petals/foil from centerpiece (third from top); bridesmaid's dress trim (bottom).

Once the paper dries, the item will be permanently embedded. If the item does not sufficiently embed, touch it up with a small dab of glue.

SMALL SCREEN METHOD

Use a mini-screen to embed heavier items, such as twigs and stemmed flowers, in specific locations.

You can make a simple mini-mold by cutting a 2" x 3" piece of brass plumbing screen. Tape a ½" width of duct tape around the edges of the screen.

After sponging a sheet on the acrylic board, place the item you wish to embed on top of the sheet. Dip the mini-mold horizontally into the vat just two to three inches, leveling it so the mini-mold is covered evenly with a thin layer of pulp. Lift it slowly, and blot lightly with a towel. Flip the mini-mold, pulp side down, onto the sheet, covering a small part of the piece you want to

Embed heavier items such as twigs or stemmed flowers using the small screen method.

embed. Press excess water from the screen's surface using a sponge. Carefully peel off the mini-mold, leaving the layer of pulp, and sponge the sheet of paper once more.

Part of your item will appear sandwiched between the main sheet of paper and the section you have applied with the mini-mold. This is much more attractive than simply gluing an item onto the paper's surface.

FLOATING MATERIALS

Use this easy floating technique to bond flat and thin materials (newspaper clippings, program pages, text, paper confetti, ribbon, tissue paper, and photocopied photographs) to a wet sheet of handmade paper. Thin and fragile natural fibers from yarn, thread, string, raffia and pressed flowers and foliage will also work, but they sometimes require a little glue once dried. Synthetic materials do not bond as well for the floating method, so instead

use the partial-embedding technique with a meat baster or small screen methods described earlier.

INSTRUCTIONS

1. Soak the item you want to float in a bowl of water (except for tissue paper, confetti, and pressed flowers or foliage, which should be used dry).
2. Place the item in the desired position on a wet piece of paper on your acrylic board before you sponge the paper for the final time.
3. Sponge the item until smooth and the remainder of the paper until the air bubbles are gone.

Use the meat baster method to embed delicate or lightweight items such as pressed bouquet ferns from the engagement party (below right) or delicate wedding flowers (left).

FRAMEABLES

Create a beautiful and lasting framed remembrance by embedding mementos around the edges of wedding photographs, poems, programs, and invitations that you've floated on handmade sheets of paper. Flattened flowers, foliage, leaves, ribbons, lace, and tulle are good choices to frame the central piece. These selected items are embedded in the paper around the edges of the floated central image after the wet sheet of paper has been placed on the acrylic sheet to dry.

INSTRUCTIONS FOR PHOTOGRAPHS

1. Make a color copy of your photo, preferably on a commercial color copying machine.

NOTE: Office-model color copiers occasionally produce copies with colors that bleed when wet, so try to use a print shop or photo-grade copier.

2. Refer to floating materials on page 88. Soak the color copy in water for about two minutes, sponge a sheet of handmade paper on your acrylic board, then place the copy on the wet sheet of paper.

3. Sponge excess water from the photocopied picture, smoothing it out.

4. Use the meat baster or small screen method of embedding to attach flat wedding mementos to the border of the photograph.

INSTRUCTIONS FOR OTHER FRAMEABLES

You can frame original programs, poems, or invitations this way, provided they aren't printed on thick paper. If the paper is thick, make a copy as you would with photographs, and follow the directions above.

Use papermaking techniques to create a priceless memento to be framed and cherished. Float an invitation, photo, poem, or program on a handmade sheet of paper, then embellish by embedding floral or other mementos around the edges.

Now that you've created a variety of wonderful papers, you can enjoy using them to make albums, scrapbooks, covered frames, and more. Prepare a special sheet of paper or use one from your collection to make the simple envelope and small gift boxes shown here.

EASY ENVELOPES

INSTRUCTIONS

1. Find a commercial envelope that will accommodate your paper sheets. Dismantle the envelope and spread open. Draw a rectangle on plain paper that snugly fits the edges of the unfolded envelope (Diagram 1).

2. Make a mold and deckle (instructions on page 78), using a screen the same size as the drawn rectangle.

3. Make the envelope paper following the instructions for papermaking beginning on page 76, except add additional pulp to the vat for each envelope sheet.

4. Once the envelope sheet is dry, lay it on a flat surface, and place the unfolded commercial envelope on top (Diagram 2).

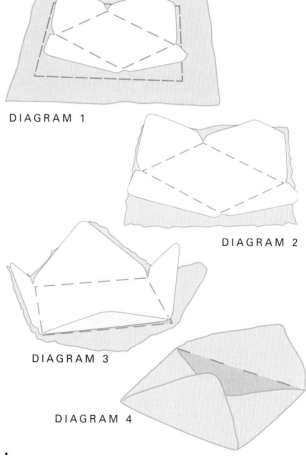

DIAGRAM 1

DIAGRAM 2

DIAGRAM 3

DIAGRAM 4

5. Fold the two together, using the creases of the commercial envelope as a guide (Diagram 3). Clip the excess paper (up to an ⅛" or so) away from the edges of your folded, handmade envelope.

6. Remove the commercial envelope and re-fold your handmade envelope (Diagram 4).

7. Use rubber cement or specific envelope glue)from papermaking suppliers) to glue the seams. Sealing wax or a sticker is enough to hold the envelope together if you do not plan to mail it.

8. For stronger envelopes, glue the commercial envelope inside.

CLASSIC SMALL GIFT BOX

With just a few folds and cuts, you can cleverly transform two flat sheets of paper into a 3-D box.

SUPPLIES *(for a 3" box)*: 8½" paper square (for top), 8¼" paper square (for bottom), pencil, scissors, ruler, glue

INSTRUCTIONS

1. Using a pencil, lightly mark an (approx.) 1½"- long X in the center of the square by aligning your ruler diagonally from corner to corner across the paper (Diagram 1).

2. Fold each of the four corners to the center of the paper (Diagram 2).

3. Fold the top and bottom edges to the center, crease and unfold (Diagram 3).

4. Fold the left and right edges to the center; crease and unfold. This gives you a small square section in each corner (Diagram 4).

5. Make cuts at top and bottom at the inside of each corner square section. Clip to fold lines (Diagram 5).

6. Pull out the points at top and bottom at the cuts and place glue near the ends of the points.

7. Bring corners A and B to the center so they meet (at dotted line), and pulled out points overlap forming the side of the box (Diagram 6). Repeat with the other two corners. Next, wrap the point sections over the top. Smooth the glued points down inside the box.

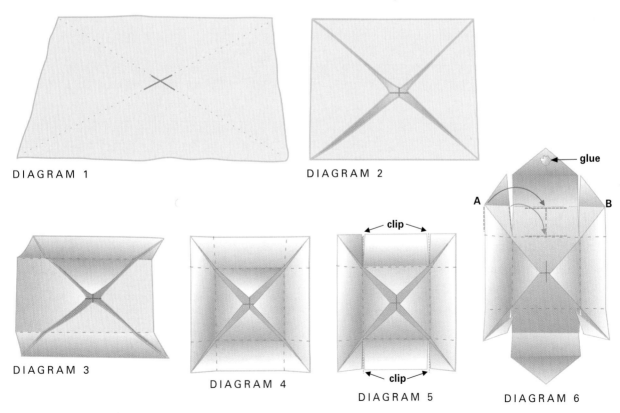

DIAGRAM 1

DIAGRAM 2

DIAGRAM 3

DIAGRAM 4

clip

clip

DIAGRAM 5

glue

A

B

DIAGRAM 6

PROBLEMS AND SOLUTIONS

Papermaking is rewarding and simple, especially if you follow the directions in this book. However, as rewarding as your results can be, unexpected problems may arise, especially if you are new to the process. The following are solutions to common problems with papermaking.

PROBLEM	SOLUTION	PREVENTION
Ink sinks into the finished paper or your pen doesn't move smoothly across the surface.	Spray the completely dried sheets with spray starch and iron them dry between sheets of parchment paper.	Add more liquid starch to the bucket of pulp before forming the sheets.
Air bubbles appear as you flip a wet sheet onto the acrylic board.	You can usually work air bubbles out by patting a sponge down on each bubble in a series of presses, moving the bubble along until it disappears out of the end of the sheet.	Sponge longer and more firmly before you remove the mold. If this doesn't work, replace your sponge with a new, highly absorbent one.
A wet sheet has folds or tears after you flip it onto the acrylic board.	Throw the sheet back into the vat, stir well, and form another sheet.	Press more firmly when you blot with the towel, to remove water from the sheet. Or you may need a new screen for your mold if yours has started to sag. The sheet may be too thin, in which case you will need to add more pulp to the vat.
The sheet's fiber is not evenly distributed. There are spots that are too thick or too thin.	Throw the sheet back into the vat, stir well, and form another sheet.	Stir the pulp in the vat longer to more thoroughly disperse the fibers. When you are forming the sheet in the vat, make sure you are taking the mold and deckle to the bottom of the vat and leveling it before you bring it up again.
Lumps of fiber appear in the wet sheet.	Throw the wet sheet back in the pulp bucket and macerate the pulp in your blender until the lumps are gone.	Macerate blender loads of pulp longer.
A wet sheet sticks to the mold or several sheets in a row have holes in the same place.	For the sticking, towel-blot the sheet several times, peel it off the mold and place it on the wet acrylic board. For the holes, use a meat baster and pulp to cover them or throw the sheet back into the vat, stir well, and form another sheet.	The screen may be clogged with pulp. Scrub the screen with a toothbrush and running water, paying special attention to the problem area.

Ellaraine Lockie is a veteran papermaker, teacher and author of The Gourmet Papermaker. *She has also published* All Because of a Button: Folklore, Fact and Fiction *as well as a collection of poetry in chapbook form, titled* Midlife Muse.

PROBLEM	SOLUTION	PREVENTION
Sheets aren't turning out as well as they have in the past.	Your mold screen may have started to sag, and you may need to replace it with a tightly stretched one. You may need to replace your sponge, as sponges lose their capacity to hold water over a period of time; a highly absorbent one is crucial.	
The edges of paper start to curl in an unsightly manner as the paper is drying on the acrylic board, producing a crinkled sheet.	If you notice the curling early, you can cover the sheet with paper towels and a heavy book. Change the paper towels as they become damp. Repeat this process until the paper is dry to the touch. Then air dry for a few more hours before removing the sheets from the acrylic board.	Spray more water on the acrylic board before you flip the sheet on it. Don't let direct sunlight reach the drying paper. Don't press as much water from the sheet when you towel blot it.
A sheet is damp on the bottom, even though it feels dry on the top, or it starts to curl after you remove it from the acrylic board.	Cover the sheet with paper towels and a heavy book and leave for a few hours. Change the paper towels as they become damp.	Leave the sheets on the acrylic board for a few hours longer—even after they feel dry.
The ends of a wet sheet have flipped over on top of the sheet.	You can occasionally separate the outer edge and move it back into place. If not, throw the sheet back into the vat and form another.	Be careful not to drag the towel across the wet sheet as you're blotting. Sponge more water from the upside-down mold onto the acrylic board before removing the mold.
The pulp smells bad.	Strain the water from the pulp and add fresh water.	Refrigerate the pulp you aren't going to use within three days or strain, label and freeze.

RESOURCES

The items used in this book are available at your local craft retailer. For specialty products consult the companies below.

SCRAPBOOK SUPPLIES

ARTIST'S MATERIALS AND PAPERS

DANIEL SMITH
4150 First Avenue South
P.O. Box 84268
Seattle, WA 98124-5568
Tel: 800-426-7640
Website: www.danielsmith.com

CUTTING SYSTEMS

FISKARS CONSUMER PRODUCTS, INC.
Home/Office/Craft
2620 Stewart Ave.
Wausau, WI 54402
Tel: 715-845-3802
Fax: 715-848-3342
Website: www.fiskars.com

COLUZZLE CUTTING SYSTEM
Creative Express
295 W. Center St.,
Provo, UT 84601
Tel: 800-563-8679
Website: www.coluzzle.com

CREATIVE MEMORIES SYSTEM
3001 Clearwater Road
P.O. Box 1839
St. Cloud, MN 56302
Tel: 800-341-5275
Website: www.creativememories.com

HANDMADE PAPER

PAPERMAKING SUPPLIERS

CARRIAGE HOUSE PAPER
79 Guernsey Street
Brooklyn, NY 11222
Tel: (718) 599-PULP; (800) 669-8781
Fax: (718) 599-7857

LEE SCOTT MCDONALD
P. O. Box 264
Charlestown, MA 02129
Tel: (617) 242-2505; (888) 627-2737
Fax: (617) 242-8825

MAGNOLIA EDITIONS
2527 Magnolia Street
Oakland, CA 94607
Tel: (510) 839-5268
Fax: (510) 893-8334

TWINROCKER
P. O. Box 413
Brookston, IN 47923
Tel: (765) 563-3119; (800) 757-8946
Fax: (765) 563-89

DYE COMPANIES

EARTH GUILD
33 Haywood Street
Asheville, NC 28801
Tel: (828) 255-7818; (800) 327-8448
Fax: (828) 255-8593
E-mail: inform@earthguild.com
catalog@earthguild.com

EARTHUES
A Natural Dye Company, Inc.
5129 Ballard Avenue NW
Seattle, WA 98107
Tel: (206) 789-1065
Fax: (206) 783-9676
Sells a natural dye instruction booklet

DHARMA TRADING CO.
P. O. Box 150916
San Rafael, CA 94915
Tel: (415) 456-7657
(800) 542-5227
Fax: (415) 456-8747
E-mail: catalog@dharmatrading.com
Website: www.dharmatrading.com

GUERRA PAINT & PIGMENT
510 E 13th Street
New York, NY 10009
Tel: (212) 529-0628
Fax: (212) 529-0787

ACKNOWLEDGMENTS

Special thanks to photographers Don Fraser (510-704-1849) and Andrew Partos (510-841-6727) of Berkeley, California. Also to photographer Stephanie Tabachnikoff, of Oakland, California, and to the many wedding parties whose inspiring images grace our pages.

Thanks also to Leslie Bond and Marcia Redford from Printed Affair, (510-654-9903), Oakland, California, for providing invitations for many of our memory album pages.

For the "Handmade Paper" chapter, thank you for permissions from: Shawn Lockie, Heather Lockie, Jenny and Chad Brix and their wedding party, Nicole and Cory Goligoski, Leslie Pelinka and Dustin Anderson, Stacey Pelinka and Jan Lustig, Kathy Bradshaw and Rosie Yacoub, Kari and Jason Shanahan, and Geary Stanley.

INDEX